ENDO[RSEMENTS]

WOW! This book holds the key to sustained, supernaturally fueled revival! The theme is just what heaven is pouring out—sacred flames of revival that burn through our hearts and our misconceptions of what God is doing on earth today. I can't think of anyone more suited to write this masterpiece than Jennifer Miskov. *Sustain the Flame* will keep you charged and challenged as we move together as one body into a global revival! Each chapter is full of insight that we need today. I'm telling you, friend, this is a brilliant book that can impact you and your ministry for eternity. The awakening winds are blowing! Catch the wind and sustain the flame!

Brian Simmons
Author of *The Passion Translation*

In *Sustain the Flame*, Jen Miskov has crafted a profound and compelling call to action, one that speaks to the very core of human existence and our relationship with the Divine. This is not a book to be taken lightly; it is a serious and thoughtful exploration of what it means to be a follower of Christ in a world that is often indifferent or even hostile to such commitments. The text is imbued with a sense of urgency and purpose, urging readers to rise above the petty squabbles and divisions that so often plague our lives and to strive for something higher—something noble and pure. The book challenges us to think deeply about our beliefs, to question our assumptions, and to strive for a level of understanding and commitment that is all too rare in today's world.

Sustain the Flame is more than a book; it is a manifesto for a way of living that is grounded in faith, love, and a deep sense of purpose. May it inspire you to rise to the challenge, embrace your God-given assignment, and keep the fire burning.

Alan DiDio
www.EncounterToday.com

I only endorse what I fully believe in—and above all, I only endorse people who are practitioners of their message. Dr. Jen Miskov is an accomplished revival historian who is unusual. Why? She is the rare historian who studies and *writes* history with her life; Jen is a revival practitioner. What you are reading is not a collection of historic memorials celebrating the "greatest hits" of revival. Moves of God in history are not meant to simply be memories we remember, but memorial stones that provoke us to do something here and now. *Sustain the Flame* is your guide to living as a burning one for Jesus all the days of your life and holds practical keys to keeping the intensity, zeal, and first-love fire for the Lord ever on the increase. *Sustain the Flame* ignites you to be the embodiment of the famous Gypsy Smith revival quote (my paraphrase): "Draw a circle, step into the circle, and ask the Lord to start revival *in that circle.*"

Larry Sparks, MDiv.
Publisher, Destiny Image
Author of *Pentecostal Fire and The Fire That Never Sleeps*
larrysparksministries.com

Jen Miskov takes us on a journey through revival history in order to define and realize revival through a beautiful mix of true stories and provoking scriptures that reveal God's plan to revive every generation. The revelation given in *Sustain The Flame* is an invaluable contribution to our generation in regard to pioneering and sustaining revival. This book is about digging deep into our intimacy with Jesus so He can light a flame in our lives that sets the world around us ablaze! Jen reveals, with exceptional insight, God's plan to revive this generation with His Spirit through unity and intimacy with Jesus.

Jen not only writes about revival, she lives it and has made sacrifices to be a living conduit for the power of God to flow through her to others. I have received many blessings through Jen's friendship and her ministry because she truly has a heart of unity and purity. Jen Miskov is a brilliant revival historian, and she is a dear friend of mine who has given her life to see the Body of Christ step into revival. We are in a season of time, a *kairos* moment, where things that were once impossible are now accessible to those who have faith eyes to see and faith ears to hear the Holy Spirit's activity. I believe this book will activate you, through guided reflection, to recognize your *kairos* moment to be a catalyst for revival.

Miriam Evans
Founder of Revival Mandate International
and Author of *Glory Miracles*

Jennifer Miskov has a passion for the presence of the precious Holy Spirit and a desire to see believers live in the awareness of that Heavenly reality. This work is the fruit of her time with the Lord and her love for God's people. I pray that you're transformed as you read *Sustain the Flame.*

David Diga Hernandez
Evangelist

Sustain the Flame by Jennifer Miskov is more than a book, it is an ignitor of hunger for unchartered new normals, and an activator of faith to fulfill the days you are made for.

Every page of this book provokes you to new levels of fiery burning and equally stirs you to radically live out the call as a sustained "living flame" unto God. It also provides prophetic insight and practical wisdom that you can easily apply to your life. You'll discover revelation keys to steward this critical season, living as a blazing furnace that ignites others and accelerates divine purpose.

If you're serious about living a radical "yes" and burning for God, this book will stir, compel, equip, mark, and commission you to run with revival fire.

Ben & Jodie Hughes
Pour It Out Ministries
Revivalists, Authors, TV Hosts

In *Sustain the Flame*, Jen writes about family as the fireplace for revival. The Bible tells us in James 1:27 that the purest and most undefiled form of religion is to care for the orphan and the widow. The reason why that is the purest and most undefiled form of religion is that it requires the church to look like its purest and undefiled form, which at its very core, is family. It's God, our Father, who adopted us all by the blood of Jesus Christ into His family. Family is truly the only context in which an orphan's needs are met.

I adopted my son Rodee when he was two years old. When he was one and a half, he was abused and shaken as an infant, which gave him cerebral palsy. When he first came to us, he was blind. The doctors said he would never connect with people and have human connections. By the love of the Father and the miraculous power of the Holy Spirit, Rodee can now see and he connects so well with people. He is my son, and he absolutely loves me, and I love him so much!

I believe that *Sustain the Flame* by Jen Miskov is going to radically impact your life. This book goes into depth about why family is the fireplace of revival and gives practical tools on how to cultivate healthy relationships around the fire of God's presence. Jen is amazing. She is a very close friend of ours. Not only her, but her entire family are good friends of ours. She is full of the Spirit. She has taken the time to research past revivals and she presents them in such a palatable way that we get to take part in, understand, and grow in because of her research, training, and ability to communicate so well. I pray that *Sustain the Flame* leads you deeper into a greater revelation of the reality that family truly is the fireplace of revival.

Michael Ketterer
Father of Six, Pediatric Mental Health Nurse, Artist

I recently had the opportunity to visit wells of revival all over Europe including Herrnhut, Germany, where God did a mighty work with the Moravians. I'm so grateful for a guide like Jen who is like a sherpa on the things we've experienced in renewal, awakening, revival as well as in the things we must lean into and pursue for further awakening and outpouring of His Spirit. In her book *Sustain the Flame* (and in our friendship), she has given words to what I've experienced personally and what I'm learning about, searching after, and pursuing in relation to revival and awakening. She's been to a place through her studies, travels, and writings where she is able to wave us over her shoulder to a place where we must go for renewal, revival, and awakening. I am so grateful for her work in *Sustain the Flame* and her friendship, and we look forward to partnering, cheering on, and seeing what God might do as He continues to pour out His Spirit on His people for such a time as this.

Zach Meerkreebs
Volunteer Soccer Coach, Asbury Outpouring 2023

SUSTAIN THE FLAME

SUSTAIN THE FLAME

*Secrets to Living Saturated
in God's Presence and Holy Fire*

JENNIFER A. MISKOV, PH.D.
with HEIDI BAKER, PH.D.

DESTINY IMAGE® PUBLISHERS, INC.
P.O. Box 310, Shippensburg, PA 17257-0310
"Publishing cutting-edge prophetic resources to supernaturally empower the body of Christ"

This book and all other Destiny Image and Destiny Image Fiction books are available at Christian bookstores and distributors worldwide.

For more information on foreign distributors, call 717-532-3040.

Reach us on the Internet: www.destinyimage.com.

ISBN 13 TP: 978-0-7684-7585-2

ISBN 13 eBook: 978-0-7684-7586-9

For Worldwide Distribution, Printed in the U.S.A.

1 2 3 4 5 6 7 8 / 28 27 26 25 24

DEDICATION

I dedicate this book to the School of Revival family. During lockdown, we found our tribe and sustained the flame together. From all parts of the globe, God brought us together to burn even more brightly for Him in the midst of a shaken world. The deep friendships that were formed, the breakthroughs that were released, the destinies that were launched, and the great comfort that was imparted in this spiritual family over the past few years is nothing short of a miracle. To you, and those in the future who will join our School of Revival family, I pray this offering is like oil poured upon the flame inside, causing it to increase and spread like wildfire for generations to come.

Set me as a seal upon your heart,

As a seal upon your arm;

For love is as strong as death,

Jealousy as cruel as the grave;

Its flames are flames of fire,

A most vehement flame.

—Song of Solomon 8:6 (NKJV)[1]

CONTENTS

GET READY

by Todd Smith

M y spirit is erupting right now. Why? Because I am moved by the words in *Sustain the Flame*. This book isn't just another book on revival—it *is* revival. Its objective is clear—to cause us to relentlessly seek the face of Jesus and to pursue His heart. Over the years Jennifer has heard, seen, and experienced the reality of the nowness of God. She is a voice that is fervently speaking to a drowsy and sleeping Church, saying, *"Come alive!"*

As I read through the chapters of this work, on many occasions I had to stop reading and gently step away from the book. I needed to pause and reflect... I couldn't go to the next paragraph because I was so captured by the Holy Spirit. He would not release me until I came to understand and grasp what I just read. On many occasions my heart was riveted with conviction. I had to pray and search my heart to make necessary adjustments. There were times I was filled with hope, fear, wonder, and faith as I considered all that God wanted to do through me if I met Him on His terms. I was left with an ever-increasing desire to go deeper and to pursue more of Him.

I can't tell you how many books I have read on the "history of revivals" and on how to "have a revival." Each one has blessed me; however, this one is different—much different! The finger of God has touched every page of this work.

Let me give you a couple of suggestions that will help you as you prepare to read *Sustain the Flame*. One, brace yourself in advance because the weight of God will settle upon you. Don't let it startle you; it is a good thing. Second, please don't be quick to turn the page. Wait. Slow down and let the hand of God descend upon you. Feel His touch and love. He has something to say to you. Turn your ear toward Him. Third, when He speaks to you, write down what He says. I have learned if you will listen to Him and understand what He is saying in the moment and then obey what you hear, God will do wonders in and through you. Again, take your time and squeeze everything out of the moments you will have with God as you read this book. Don't be in a hurry.

Here at Christ Fellowship Church in Dawsonville, Georgia—the host church of the North Georgia Revival—we have witnessed tens of thousands of people who have traveled from all over the world to encounter Jesus in our baptismal waters. Thousands of miracles, salvations, and healings have taken place right before our eyes. I truly believe we are in a move of God. However, even though I am living in revival, this book has challenged me deeply and has stirred my soul to pursue Him even more vigorously. The same will happen to you!

Prepare yourself for and embrace the journey that lies ahead. Trust me, you will not be the same. It will be so worth it!

Pastor Todd Smith
Lead Pastor Christ Fellowship Church, Dawsonville, GA
Host Pastor of the North Georgia Revival

PART 1

BORN FOR SUCH
A TIME AS THIS

You were born to be a gift of God for this generation. The tsunami wave of revival long prophesied is already upon us. God has entrusted us with this *kairos* moment. He is calling us to become spiritual mothers and fathers who can steward this end-time harvest. The time to dive into the fresh move of the Spirit is upon us.

DEEPER

by Heidi Baker

God is inviting you deeper into the river of living waters. He wants to take you past your ankles, past your knees, past your waist, and in over your head. He wants to drown you in His love. He wants to take you so deep in Him that you begin to experience a completely different reality, to live in a different realm. The veil is thin. It can become so thin that there are moments where we can sense what it might be like for those who have gone ahead of us. We know that they are full of joy unspeakable. The presence of the King is very close.

There is a river that flows from the throne of God and of the Lamb down through the great streets of the new Jerusalem (Revelation 22). It is living water for the kingdom on earth and also for the kingdom above. All around it are those who have gone ahead and are face to face with Jesus (Hebrews 12:1–2). There is no fear there. There is no sorrow or suffering. There is a cloud of witnesses. Their testimony calls us deeper and closer.

Though going deep in the Holy Spirit and the river of God's glory-love may frighten us, the cloud of witnesses is saying to us, "Do not fear. There is a *kairos* moment upon us. It's time. Beyond your own understanding, beyond the veil—it's time to dive in."

CHAPTER 1

DIVING IN

You are not here by accident. You are chosen by God to be set apart, consumed by the fire of His love. If you are reading this right now, I believe you are a part of the remnant army of Jesus lovers He is raising up for such a time as this. God is inviting you to step into your calling as a burning one for Him who will finish well. This book is a call to pursue Jesus with total abandonment and to partner in covenantal unity with the body of Christ to keep the fires of revival burning for generations to come.

There is a massive tsunami wave of revival increasingly coming upon us. It has already begun and is building. Just as a tidal wave gets bigger the closer it gets to land, so this next move of God builds upon the momentum of centuries past. We are riding in the spiritual currents of the early Church of Acts, Martin Luther and the Protestant Reformation, the Moravians, John Wesley and the Great Awakening, Charles Finney, the Welsh Revival, the Azusa Street Revival, the Jesus People Movement, and many more. The cloud of witnesses is cheering us on! We are not just building on one of these revivals; we are riding on the accumulated momentum of them all. There is great synergy of the ages that will propel us into a greater dimension of God's glory than in times past.[1]

As we step into what God has for us in our generation, it will also be important to position ourselves to steward this revival well.[2] If we want to ride this wave of revival to the fullest, we need to prioritize investing in kingdom relationships. We need to be vigilant to both fill our lamps with the oil of intimacy and become reconciled and unified with our brothers and sisters in Christ.[3] Intimacy with Jesus alongside covenant relationships within the body of Christ are crucial for the fires of revival to be sustained. The synergy of the ages is upon us with a mighty outpouring of the Holy Spirit like we have never seen before, along with increased persecution.[4] We need to intentionally prepare for this intensification now.

If we are not deeply rooted in Christ as our Source, grounded in His Word, and fortified together with the family of God, as this massive wave increases in all its fullness, though it is marvelous, it can take us out if we are not properly prepared. This book was written to help make you ready, so that you are not crushed under the heavy, weighty glory of God, derailed by increasing favor, or taken out by the enemy as the tide rises. My heart is to awaken, equip, and call you into your God-given assignment for such a time as this (see Ephesians 2:10). My desire is that you will be so established in your relationship with Christ and unified with His body that you will be prepared to ride this epic wave in all its glory and will be able to carry that momentum forward.

Unity commands a blessing, increases anointing, and positions us to steward revival well.[5] We need each other. We can't do this alone. We must lay aside all contentions, offenses, and divisions for the unifying purpose of glorifying Jesus and making His name known. It is time to "plunge" into the deep end of the waters of the Holy Spirit both "individually and collectively," as Frank Bartleman, eyewitness and intercessor, once wrote. He encourages us today just as he did over a hundred years ago in the early days of the Azusa Street Revival when he wrote:

> Opportunity once passed, is lost forever. There is a time when the tide is sweeping by our door. We may then plunge in and be carried to glorious blessing, success and

victory. To stand shivering on the bank, timid, or paralyzed with stupor, at such a time, is to miss all, and most
miserably fail, both for time and for eternity. Oh, our
responsibility! The mighty tide of God's grace and favor is
even now sweeping by us, in its prayer-directed course....
It is time to "get together," and plunge in, individually and
collectively. We are baptized "in one Spirit, into one body,"
- I Cor. 12:13. Let us lay aside all carnal contentions and
divisions, that separate us from each other and from God.
If we are of His body, we are "one body." The opportunity
of a lifetime, of centuries, is at our door, to be eternally
gained or lost. There is no time to hesitate. Act quickly,
lest another take thy crown. Oh, church of Christ, awake!
Be baptized with power. Then fly to rescue others. And to
meet your Lord.[6]

CHAPTER 2

SURF LESSONS

There is something about being in the water and riding waves that makes me come alive. It's one of my greatest passions. From the time I was thirteen years old, I grew up bodyboarding the waves at Newport Beach, California. After decades of being in the ocean on a regular basis, I have learned to study the elements to predict when the waves will be good.

Most avid surfers also become skilled researchers. There are many different factors that need to come into alignment for the waves to be good: swell size and direction, wind speed and direction, atmospheric pressure, shape of the land, tidal push or pull, and the list goes on. South swells make some beaches come alive while entirely missing north-facing beaches. When all the elements come into alignment for the waves to be good at a certain break, if one is prepared to show up at the right time, that person will score great waves. Sometimes this means rearranging schedules, missing work, or doing whatever is necessary to capitalize on the unique moment. Epic waves don't work around our plans; we must adapt to their flow. The worst thing to hear when paddling out is that the waves were amazing *yesterday*.

There are also times when a person walks into a divine moment without even knowing it. And they still must make a choice. I had one of these moments early in the summer of 2020 when I went on a road trip up the coast of California for a silent retreat in a monastery. Of course,

I packed my bodyboard and wetsuit and stopped by several beaches on the way up, checking out the waves to see if I might find something fun to ride. None of the spots looked like what I was hoping for.

I randomly took an exit off the freeway and when I pulled into a beach parking lot, I somehow stumbled upon a sweet little wedge wave with only a few guys out. It was around 1 p.m., and I had been driving all morning. I was ready to get wet. Yet I still had a choice: Do I just watch the other surfers because I was not a local there, the water was freezing, and I had to check in at the monastery soon? Or do I seize the day, take hold of this unique moment in time that would never be repeated, and have a quick little session? Thank God I decided to paddle out because the waves were super fun. The side wave produced speed for big maneuvers. Yes, the water was freezing, but this ended up being one of the best sessions I'd had in a very long time. What if I hadn't recognized the special moment before my eyes and gone into the water?

While this example is not a life-or-death situation, I share this story to demonstrate that there are moments in time when we must capture the present opportunity, or we can miss out. The wave of revival is going to break either way; the question is, are we going to be in position and prepared to ride it when it comes? When I arrived at the beach that day, the tide was low going to high. Because it was at a unique time, there weren't many surfers out, and I was able to catch a few epic waves. If I had arrived earlier in the day, the wave would not have been breaking quite like it was, because the tide would have been different, and there likely would have been more surfers out. On my way back down from Big Sur, I chose not to surf anywhere along the way because I wanted to get back to this special spot. The only problem was that when I arrived, the tide was different, the swell had died down, and it wasn't breaking at all. Looking back, I am so thankful I paddled out on my way up, because it was a special time when all the elements came together so perfectly. I knew it was one of those *kairos* moments—a gift from God.[1]

CHAPTER 3

KAIROS

During a *kairos* season, things accelerate at a rapid pace. Possibilities that were not available ten years earlier suddenly come within reach. *Kairos* is the Greek word in the New Testament for "time." It is also translated as "the right time, a set time, opportunity, due season, short time, the time when things are brought to crisis, and the decisive epoch waited for."[1] It can also mean a divinely appointed time. It is used for purpose, value, and being present in a moment of destiny. The following Scriptures use the word *kairos* to describe time.[2]

> *"The **time** [kairos] has come," he said. "The kingdom of God has come near. Repent and believe the good news!"*
>
> Mark 1:15

> *From one man he made all the nations, that they should inhabit the whole earth; and he marked out their appointed times [kairos] in history and the boundaries of their lands.*
>
> Acts 17:26

> *For he says,*
> *"In the **time** [kairos] of my favor I heard you,*
> *and in the day of salvation I helped you."*

> *I tell you, now is the time* [kairos] *of God's favor, now is the*
> *day of salvation.*
>
> 2 Corinthians 6:2

Seizing the day. Bringing in the harvest. Moses, Esther, Joseph, and others being born for such a *time* as this. Our stepping into this unique moment in history—all these things tie into the theme of *kairos* time.[3]

It is also interesting to note that there are several consistencies with *kairos* time being linked to the harvest, or even being translated as "harvest time."[4] Figuratively, harvest time can mean the act of gathering people into the kingdom of God. Here is one example of harvest paired with a *kairos* moment.

> *Let both grow together until the **harvest**. At that **time** [kai-*
> *ros] I will tell the **harvesters**: First collect the weeds and tie*
> *them in bundles to be burned; then gather the wheat and*
> *bring it into my barn.*
>
> Matthew 13:30

Might there be a specific God-appointed time to bring in the harvest like it says in Matthew 13:30? Maybe there is an important reason *kairos* is regularly tied to the harvest. Perhaps God has been waiting all along to bring in this end-time harvest of souls with one concentrated sweep into His kingdom.

WINDOW OF OPPORTUNITY

A *kairos* moment can also be described as a window of opportunity. There is an anointing upon a *kairos* season in a heightened way. More is possible, accessible, and accelerated during that time than before. Revival becomes more potent and available in *kairos* time. We also have the choice in how much we will participate in what He is doing in these seasons. God sets apart these special times and gives us the keys to unlock His kingdom.

If *kairos* represents a special window of opportunity, when that window closes, a special grace comes to an end. The Israelites were freed from bondage in Egypt with radical signs and wonders, including watching the Red Sea part before their eyes (Exodus 14). God led them with a cloud by day and fire by night. Then they had a window of opportunity, a *kairos* moment, to step into their Promised Land. Joshua and Caleb came back with a faith-filled report birthed through the lens of God's perspective (Numbers 14). The other ten spies spread doubt throughout the camp because they saw through the eyes of fear. They chose instead to focus on the circumstances rather than see with the eyes of faith. The Israelites then had a choice to make in this window of opportunity. Would they immediately respond to God's invitation to take the land, keeping their eyes on Him and trusting in Him, or shrink back?

Instead of stepping into all that God had for them in this special *kairos* moment, the Israelites partnered with fear and hesitated to move forward. Later when they attempted to obey God's command, that window of opportunity had closed. It was too late. Their delayed obedience was actually disobedience, and it caused a whole generation to die off, forfeiting their inheritance. They missed out. It was a tragic loss, and they were never given that opportunity again.[5]

There are times when we need to hear the truth that no matter what, we can't miss out on our destinies because there is grace, and God will eventually get us to where we need to be. Other times, we need to hear the truth that we *can* miss out on the fullness of what He has for us if we hesitate and fail to respond to His leading in a moment. I believe the *rhema* "now word" we must heed is that our moment of opportunity is upon us, and if we don't step into the flow of the Holy Spirit's momentum in this unique season, we can miss out on all He has for us. There is an urgency to step into all He has for us today, so it doesn't pass us by. If we fail to move where He is leading in this hour, we may have to painfully wait and watch our generation die off before God can raise up a new remnant who will swiftly respond to His leading to step into all that He has for them. Or, if we choose to sit back rather than dive in, the wave will likely still come, but we may have to watch from the sidelines as those with a yielded "yes" pioneer the next move of God in front of our eyes.

WE ARE IN A *KAIROS* MOMENT

The early twentieth century was pregnant with revival in a *kairos* moment. Revival broke out in Wales in 1904–05, in India in 1905, and then in Los Angeles in 1906 at Azusa Street, in addition to other world-wide moves all around the same time.[6] There was something anointed, set apart, and special about this divine season that these saints were able to recognize and tap into. Many great revivals birthed during that small window of time are still impacting us today.

Our generation is also experiencing another *kairos* moment over one hundred years later. After the world got hit with the 2020 Covid-19 pandemic and global lockdown, many of us felt like the barren sand when the tide pulls back before a huge tsunami wave crashes in. Everything not stable enough to stand on its own has been stripped away. I began writing this book before 2020 and ended up finishing it in 2023. During the time the world shut down, I birthed School of Revival in May 2020, and then in September 2022, stepped into my Miracle House, which you will hear about later. In February 2023, I also had the opportunity to visit the Asbury Revival that broke out in Wilmore, Kentucky, when less than twenty students lingered in worship after a chapel service.[7] We are alive in a unique moment of history. God is accelerating things in this *kairos* season like never before.

GOD HAS ENTRUSTED US WITH THIS *KAIROS* MOMENT

It is essential we understand the season we are in. We must become like the people from Issachar, "who understood the times and knew what Israel should do" (1 Chronicles 12:32).

Since the beginning of time, God purposed that *we* would be alive for such a time as this. He has entrusted *us* with this unique moment in history to steward both the challenges and the outpourings of our day. No other generation has been entrusted to bring hope, light, and healing following 2020. We have been given a unique opportunity to partner with Him to bring solutions to the world's problems, to preach the gospel to those who are now open to receive, and to ride on the momentum of the many accumulated wells of revival now opened all at the same time. God has positioned us to be in perfect alignment for what He's pouring out all around us—His Spirit and new wine in unprecedented measures.

We are at a turning point, a precipice, a point of decision. How we respond in this *kairos* moment will determine if we step into the fullness of our God-given destiny as a generation or not. The window of opportunity to lead our generation into all God has for us will not stay open forever. There is a line drawn in the sand. Today, if we so desire, we can step across the threshold into greater depths of the Spirit. There is a move of God upon us, with an open invitation to all who are willing to get in position and dive in.

That's why you are here. God is filling you with faith like Joshua and Caleb's to inspire this generation to step into its destiny. He is igniting a fresh fire in you that will set many others ablaze for Him. He is raising you up as a spiritual mother or father to help steward this incoming end-time harvest and to bring new believers into the family. The hour has come. The time to step in is now.

Lord, help us to see and understand the unique *kairos* moment You have entrusted us with. May we steward this time well and advance Your kingdom so that generations who come after us will ride on the momentum we paved the way for them to have. In Jesus' name, amen.

QUESTIONS FOR REFLECTION

What does it look like for you to step into all that God has for you in this *kairos* moment? As you reflect on your personal history, what other *kairos* moments can you identify in your own life? What are some of the prophetic words, visions, dreams, revelations, or blessings that have been spoken over you or given to you? How can you position yourself now to prepare to steward the weight of your calling as God continues to unfold it in its fullest measure?

CHAPTER 4

ESTABLISHING CULTURE

A s we navigate in this *kairos* moment to see God pour out His Spirit like never before, it is important to remember that keeping our lamps full of the oil of intimacy with Jesus is essential for being a revival-fire carrier (Matthew 25:1–12). Without oil, the fire burning inside will wane. In two of my previous books, *Walking on Water* (2017) and *Fasting for Fire* (2021), I talk more about how to cultivate personal intimacy with Jesus by staying full of the oil of His presence. Now we will build upon that foundation with another important aspect of stewarding the fire: surrounding ourselves with other burning ones who are sold out for Jesus.

As we move toward building healthy covenant relationships, note that this book directly builds off chapter 9: "Preparing to Steward the Next Great Awakening" of my book *Ignite Azusa: Positioning for a New Jesus Revolution* (2016).[1] If you get the chance, I highly encourage you to read that to learn more of the context and momentum leading into this book. While *Ignite Azusa* looks at the Azusa Street Revival (1906) more in-depth, that specific revival will only be mentioned here. I believe the following excerpts from chapter 9 of this book foreshadow where we find ourselves in this season.[2]

"CREATING A CULTURE TO STEWARD THE BILLION-SOUL HARVEST"

Today, we have been given an incredible opportunity to create a new normal for what this next generation and beyond can be. Imagine what future generations will look like if those from this incoming billions-soul harvest get born into a family of burning Jesus-lovers who are marked by intimacy, signs, wonders, love, and family. Whatever culture we welcome the flood of new believers into will become their normal. That's why one of the questions we need to ask is, what kind of culture do we want these new believers to be born into?

Many of us have spent years building our relationship with Christ. We have invested countless hours worshiping at Jesus' feet and simply being with Him. We have deepened our relationship with Christ by connecting with Him in prayer, fasting, and reading the Word. We have invested time, energy, and even resources to learn how to prophesy, grow in greater faith to step out to heal the sick, and to follow the leading of the Spirit at all costs. But what if when the new harvest comes, our ceiling becomes their floor? What if these newly converted ones get born into a family marked by intimacy with Jesus and revival fire? What if prayer, fasting, and reading God's Word become their starting point and new normal? What will happen if those from this billions-soul harvest get invited into a family of believers who do life centered on the presence of God and who also do great exploits for the kingdom together? What does it look like to have someone born into a culture that stewards intimacy with Jesus and is committed to the body of Christ in love? We have the opportunity to shape what the next era of Christianity will look like and to partner with heaven to create a new wineskin for the new wine that's about to be poured out.[3]

"FAMILY: THE FIREPLACE FOR REVIVAL"

One of the greatest movements in history that contributed to the rapid spread of Christianity began when God crashed in on a handful of family and friends who were hungry for more of God. The Azusa Street Revival began as the "Bonnie Brae Street Revival" before it contributed to the spread of global Pentecostalism. The fruit that was released from this little tribe of less than twenty people who gathered in a home on Bonnie Brae Street is incredible.[4] There is something significant about seeking God together with friends and inviting Him to invade even the intimate spaces of family.

Revival begins and is sustained in family. In this next era, Christianity will burst forth from the seams of churches, communities, homes, families, and intimate spaces and be carried over into the world. The Sunday worship celebrations will be important to testify and share more widely about what God is doing in the city, the region, and the nations. The place of more intimate connection will also need to be cultivated in smaller communities as more people enter the family of God.

Being intentional with community will be an important factor in stewarding this next move of God like it was for those at Azusa. Doing life together with a small tribe of our people will be an important aspect of stewarding and discipling this incoming harvest. Staying known in a close-knit community with others who burn for Jesus is a key for sustaining revival and finishing well. Evan Roberts, leader of the Welsh Revival, isolated himself many times from community, and the revival died down shortly after. Cultivating healthy community is important for continuing to burn—and to not burn out.

We need each other to fulfill our truest destiny. There are keys to our destiny that are hidden within the lives and hearts of those whom God has positioned us to run with in each season. The way to access these keys in each other is to intentionally do life together, be vulnerable, love each other well, and go after the things of God together.

As we begin to go after praying for stadiums full of people being saved, at the same time, we need to realize the importance of going deeper with the few. We can only be close with a handful of people at one time. Jesus had the twelve, but then He also had Peter, James, and John, with John as His most intimate friend. They lived together, traveled together, ate together, ministered together, and did life together.

There is something important about doing life together in God's presence. Close community was crucial to the beginnings of the Azusa Street Revival just as it was for Jesus in His ministry. Homes represent intimate spaces of family and deep friendships. It's easy to blend in with the crowd in larger settings and slip out without really letting anyone in. People can't hide or avoid the deeper things of the heart in a home or small community.

The keys to our destiny are found in intimacy with Jesus and in family. Besides the Moravian community in Herrnhut, Germany, there were also those in the Jesus People Movement who opened community houses for the new believers. The family of believers hosts the fire of God in a greater way than an individual can do alone.[5]

SPIRITUAL PARENTING

After reading these portions of *Ignite Azusa*, it is easy to see there is an even greater need *today* to raise up spiritual mothers and fathers than ever before. New believers need to be welcomed into the family of God, so they are not lost or taken out by the enemy. Many previous revivals waned too quickly or produced knee-deep Christians or those who would later walk away from their faith, largely because of a lack of discipleship and spiritual parenting. Many baby Christians were left "orphaned" in the faith. John Wesley observed the dangers of revival without discipleship:

I was more convinced than ever that preaching like an apostle, without joining together those that are awakened and training them up in the ways of God, is only begetting children for the murderer. How much preaching has there been for these twenty years all over Pembrokeshire! But no regular societies, no discipline, no order or connection, and the consequence is that nine in ten of the once-awakened are now faster asleep than ever.[6]

We must take seriously the need to enfold, disciple, and adopt newly born or awakened believers so their fire does not get snuffed out.

The most important things in life are not things or ministry or success; they are people. Relationship goes beyond strategies and structures. If we want to steward this next move of God well, we need to not only disciple the incoming harvest so they are deep rooted, but we also need to mother and father them in the Spirit as well. There needs to be intentionality in building these connections and going deeper together, and covenant will play an important role in our upcoming perspective on kingdom relationships.

It is important that we welcome new believers into a healthy revival culture of family stewarded around the presence of God. These "newborns" in the Spirit will need mothers and fathers to raise them up in the ways of the Lord. Stepping into our rightful place as spiritual parents in the faith, we can train, equip, love, and adopt newborns of the kingdom.

We don't need to disciple a stadium full of people, but we do need to welcome the few God brings to us. Connection to the family of God and investing in the few have the power to change the world. Jesus did this with the twelve. Who knows what would happen if everyone reading this book spiritually "adopted" the few God highlights in this season? While there may be patterns and best practices for stewarding the incoming harvest that we can learn from the Moravians and others, at the core of doing this well is cultivating a bond of love, connection, and covenant in family. It's not about building strategies or models; it's about building people because God's kingdom looks like family.

It seems to me that in American Christianity and beyond, in some ways, the conference circuit has taken over. My fear is that we have created a construct that feeds consumer Christianity and doesn't lend toward discipling or spiritual parenting people deeply. There can be value in going somewhere to receive impartation from time to time, but it's the engrained rhythm and overconsumption by conference hoppers that worries me for what we are building into future generations. I often participate in conferences and know that many have had radical encounters with God in these environments, but I just wonder if that is the only model. Might there be a new wineskin God wants to introduce more aimed at building healthy spiritual family? I wonder what would happen if smaller retreats, open houses, family-style dinners, and intimate home worship gatherings became more of the new normal in the coming years. I wonder what new wineskins God wants to introduce into our generation for establishing people in spiritual family.

You were born for a purpose in this *kairos* moment. God has given you keys to the kingdom and creative solutions for every problem you face. The momentum of the ages is upon us. Many have paid a price to get us the freedom and knowledge we now have. We need the family of God to help form us into who we are meant to be, so we can step into our God-given destiny as a generation. We also need to become the family of God to each other in a greater way, so that generations are not lost.

QUESTIONS FOR REFLECTION

Is there anyone God is highlighting to you to take under your wing— someone He has given you a special grace for? What does it look like for you to invite God into the intimate space of your home and family in a greater measure today?

PART 2

FAMILY IS THE FIREPLACE OF REVIVAL

Everything flows from our relationship with God and with each other. It is in the context of family that we need to learn to steward the fires of revival, so these flames continue to burn and can be passed on for generations to come. In this section, we will take a closer look at how family is the fireplace of revival and prepare to see this truth lived out more fully in our lives.

NOT ORPHANS

by Heidi Baker

So much of the time, we in the Church act as if we are orphans taking care of other orphans. But it is not God's will that we should forever live in orphanages. He wants homes! Homes, full of family and loving believers. The Church is not called to be like an orphanage, because none of us are called to be orphans. The Church is a forever-family. It's an eternal home. We're created to share our lives generously and joyously with each other, because Abba is our one Father, and Jesus is our one King.

The Holy Spirit has been given to the Church so that everyone may be adopted, not just in name but in reality. The Holy Spirit makes all things new. Jesus will give you a renewed heart, so that you can be at one with His family, so that you can be brought in and bring others in and love them as yourself. His family does not need to compete against each other. Why would a child who is fully loved have to compete with another child who is also fully loved? When you know who you are in Christ, you will not think of competing for love.

He wants to take every trace of an orphan spirit from us. In His kingdom there is a special anointing for every single son and every single daughter. There is a holy presence beyond anything we have yet known. There is food and drink at the table. As we have been invited, so we invite others.

The Lord wants to lift up our eyes to see the great harvest waiting before us. He is not sending us to the harvest as orphans. He is sending us as sons and daughters, with provision in our hands. He will give us whatever we need for the journey. If we will release the reins to Him, we will mount up on wings like eagles. We will run and not grow weary, walk and not faint. God has given each of us fresh bread to carry, and many millions of souls are hungry for it. We must remain fully filled and go to them, with washed feet, clean hands, and pure hearts.

CHAPTER 5

FAMILY

I remember getting the call while I was at work. My grandpa was going to die very soon. My family was getting ready to drive an hour to the nursing home to be with him for his final moments. It was 2004, and as the assistant manager at Starbucks, I was working my shift with one other person. I knew I couldn't leave him at the store alone. I also knew how hard it was to get someone to cover my shift at the last minute. My manager later offered to come in to cover my shift, but I didn't want to be a burden. Also, just the thought of all my family being emotional in a room made me feel uncomfortable. At that point in my life, I wasn't used to pain or loss or expressing emotions much, and I had only a few minutes to make the decision. I ended up staying at work to finish my shift to spare everyone the hassle.

I was an emotional wreck the whole afternoon, while everyone in the family but me got to surround my grandpa and be there for his final breath. Some told me later how special it was to be present for that sacred transition into heaven. I knew I had missed out, and I have always regretted not being there.

Decades earlier, when I was about three weeks old, my father nearly died. On March 10th, a few days after his thirty-seventh birthday, he woke up around three in the morning and noticed his lower body from his waist down was becoming numb. My mom was awake breastfeeding me at that time. They decided he should try to take a warm bath to feel better. Since there was no change, he drove himself to the emergency room nearby and told my mom that he'd be right back. When he arrived at the hospital, he was not able to sign his name on the form, so they helped him make an "X" for the signature. He was quickly becoming paralyzed. The doctors called my mom later that day to update her and let her know they were doing tests to find out what was wrong.

My dad was in an isolation intensive care unit because they didn't know what was happening and didn't want anyone to catch a contagious virus if that was the issue. When my mom first arrived there, they made her dress head to toe in protective hospital gown and attire. When she wasn't at the hospital, she was at home with me, a newborn, and my siblings: my brother, who was two-and-a-half years old, and my older sister, who was fourteen. My parents immediately decided to pull my older sister out of school so she could help take care of me and my brother so that my mom could go back and forth to the hospital.

Three days after my dad was admitted to the hospital, the doctor called my mom. She was upstairs in her bedroom holding me in her arms at the time. He told her that my dad was going to die or be in a wheelchair for the rest of his life. When she hung up the phone, with me still in her arms, the thought crossed her mind to jump out of the window. Thankfully, instead of responding to the enemy's voice, in desperation she called out to God for help and prayed that my dad would be healed.

Less than five minutes later, someone knocked on the door. One of my mom's friends named Margaret just happened to be in the neighborhood at that exact time and wanted to stop by to see "baby Jenny." That was me! My sister updated her on things with my dad. Then she asked to come upstairs to see my mom and offered to pray for her. My mom thought she would go home to pray, but instead she sat my mom down on the bed with me in her arms and prayed for us right there. That was the first time my mom had ever received prayer like that. She also offered to help my mom in any way possible.

The next day while Margaret was helping my mom do deliveries for my dad's business, her husband Sam went to visit my dad in the hospital. The hospital wasn't allowing visitors because of the severity of my dad's condition and all the unknowns. The only people allowed to see him were immediate family. When Sam checked in at the hospital, he said he was my dad's brother. What he really meant was he was his "brother in Christ." It worked—he was in. After putting on a hospital gown, mask, and booties, he arrived in my dad's room and asked if he could pray for him. This was the first time my dad had ever received prayer by the laying on of hands. This was also the first time Sam had stepped out in faith to pray for someone like this.

Even with all the prayers, however, there was still no improvement. As the days stretched on, my mom wondered if she would end up widowed and have to raise her kids as a single parent. The doctors soon found out my dad had transverse myelitis, which is an inflammation of the spinal cord. To this day, they still do not know what causes this disease. Once they discovered what was wrong, they moved him into a regular intensive care unit and other family members and friends were finally able to visit him. They were told to remain positive while with him, but many became emotional in the hallway after seeing him in such a state. My dad didn't know the severity of all that was going on because he was never in any pain. Eventually the hospital allowed him to see me and my brother and sister in the lobby, but he wasn't even able to hold me because of the paralysis.

A couple of weeks later, there *still* wasn't any improvement. Then Easter Sunday came. That evening, a Chinese nurse came in to turn him over in the bed to prevent bed sores. She started to sing hymns over him as she rubbed his back. He fell asleep that night, and when he awoke the following morning, he could move his fingers and toes! Feeling began to increase in the rest of his body as well. The doctors had no idea how he recovered.

They all said it was a *miracle*.

My dad never saw that nurse again. Was she an angel? Well, whatever you want to believe, but from that moment on, my dad's healing journey began. He had to go through physical therapy for six weeks to relearn how to walk, but he was eventually fully restored. It's crazy to think that right when I came into the world, there was a chance that I could have grown up without a father—but God. But God intervened and healed him, and I've been blessed with the gift of a great dad throughout my life.

My father's love, presence, and support over the years has shaped the way I look at my heavenly Father. I have always had a great and trusting relationship with God the Father because of the love I received from my earthly father. I know this is not the case for everyone, but God also is a Redeemer for those whose stories look different.

Our family culture lays the foundation for how we do life. This book is a story about family. This is not just a story about the importance of family, but how our family extends to the body of Christ and how we need each other if we want to step into the fullness of all God has for us. We were never meant to walk this Christian life alone. We need each other to help steward the flame within.

My dad holding me up after he was healed, with my grandpa in
the background.

DEFINING FAMILY

With one of our goals being to learn how to steward revival in a healthy spiritual family where there are no orphans, let's first add some context and attempt to define terms. In Christian circles, the term *family* is thrown around regularly. But if everyone has a different understanding of what family looks like, it will be hard to go on the same journey together. Let's add some clarity and parameters here.

When I talk about family in this book, I am mainly referring to the family of God, the body of Christ, our spiritual family, the big C global Church. This can and hopefully does include a person's physical family as well, but it does not have to. For many, there may be pain tied to the term *family* because of past hurts. Some may have been neglected or not treated well, or they may have even been abused by someone in their family. If that is your case, please try to see this term in a new light as you read this book. See it in relation to your true spiritual family found in the body of Christ. Or, if you've been hurt by the church, as many have, see this term according to its redemptive nature as the glorious bride God calls us to become together as one. In our context, family can also be seen as a smaller group within the whole, or a tribe within a tribe. The Israelites were God's chosen people, but within the wider community, there were twelve tribes, and within the twelve tribes, there were smaller clans composed of individual families.

FAMILY IS KINGDOM

As we go on this journey together, you will see how the fires of revival are ignited, sustained, and increase in the context of spiritual family. Family is the fireplace of revival. If you want to discover the kingdom of God, it is found in family. The Lord's Prayer starts with "Our Father" and ends with "Yours is the kingdom" (Matthew 6:9–13 NKJV). The kingdom of God has a Father. The Trinity are three in one, working together in perfect unity as family: God the Father, Jesus the Son, and the Holy Spirit. God is also the Father who sent His only Son for us. Since He is our Father, that means we are His children. Thus, we are all brothers and sisters in Christ. The kingdom of God in its purest form is manifested as family.

BECOMING A DWELLING PLACE

To cultivate a healthy spiritual family, we need intimate space to connect at a heart level. We can't nurture deep kingdom relationships in a large crowd. We can only do it in a smaller environment where we spend enough time together to be known. Healthy community is where people are seen, known, and loved and—as a result—are regularly healed, restored, and catalyzed into their destinies. This tends to happen in a more intimate space or a household.

God models this beautifully for us by making us members of His household. In Ephesians 2:19–22, Paul says:

> *Consequently, you are no longer foreigners and strangers, but fellow citizens with God's people and also members of his household, built on the foundation of the apostles and prophets, with Christ Jesus himself as the chief cornerstone. In him the whole building is joined together and rises to become a holy temple in the Lord. And in him you too are being built together to become a dwelling in which God lives by his Spirit.*

What an incredible privilege we get as the body of Christ to be joined together to steward His glory and become a dwelling place for the Most High. It is almost too wonderful to grasp that the Creator of the universe would want to come and dwell within us. As the family of God, we are living stones being built together as a dwelling place where He lives by His Spirit (1 Peter 2:5). He wants to build a place not only of visitation but of *habitation*, where He can come and dwell. Now that is radical.

If family is the fireplace of revival and God is a consuming fire, then a family of believers gathered around His presence is key to sustaining the fires of revival. One flame standing alone may eventually wane, but when multiple flames get together, an inferno erupts. Together we are to become the fireplace that houses the fire of God's incoming presence and keeps the flame burning, so it can continue for generations to come. From this fireplace of family, the flames can also be sent out around the world to ignite other fires of revival.

QUESTIONS FOR REFLECTION

What has your experience been with your own family? What has your experience with the family of God looked like? Are there any areas that God wants to heal, restore, or reframe in relation to family and the body of Christ so you can have a healthy perspective of cultivating revival in family?

CHAPTER 6

FIRE

L et's explore what *fire* can represent in relation to our context. Hebrews 12:28–29 says:

> *Therefore, since we are receiving a kingdom that cannot be shaken, let us be thankful, and so worship God acceptably with reverence and awe, for our "God is a consuming fire."*

Ultimately, when referring to fire throughout this book, we are talking about the fiery presence of God Himself. Fire can also specifically represent the Holy Spirit. John the Baptist said that One was coming after him who would baptize with the Holy Spirit and fire (Matthew 3:11). When the day of Pentecost had fully come, the Holy Spirit appeared as fire and rested on the disciples' heads in the upper room (Acts 2:1–4).

Fire can represent the glory of God. When Moses was on top of the mountain in God's glory, the Israelites looked up and saw a consuming fire (Exodus 24:16–18). Fire can also represent the flames in Jesus' eyes, as described in Revelation 19:12. We can feel the fire of God burning in our hearts the way the two men walking closely with Jesus on the road to Emmaus experienced it (Luke 24:13–35). Fire can be used in relation to consecration and refinement, purifying us to see God more clearly and to become yielded vessels for Him.[1] In Song of Songs 8:6–7 (TPT), we see that fire can be used to describe the intensity of the intimate burning love God has for us:

Fasten me upon your heart as a seal of fire forevermore.
This living, consuming flame
will seal you as my prisoner of love.
My passion is stronger
than the chains of death and the grave,
all consuming as the very flashes of fire
from the burning heart of God.
Place this fierce, unrelenting fire over your entire being.
Rivers of pain and persecution
will never extinguish this flame.
Endless floods will be unable
to quench this raging fire that burns within you.
Everything will be consumed.
It will stop at nothing
as you yield everything to this furious fire
until it won't even seem to you like a sacrifice anymore.

Fire can also be used to describe the flames of revival. Revival fire is when we have become revived to Jesus as our first love and are burning to know Him more (Revelation 2:4). For our purposes here, fire will represent the increased manifest presence of God in its powerful purifying form. Those found at the heart of God's radiant presence live fully alive and become catalytic for revival fire to spread through their lives. They live with the flame Himself.

LIVING IN THE FIRE

It is important that we learn to cultivate a lifestyle of remaining on fire in our love for Jesus, so that we can be agents who release revival. Without the fire of God's presence, we have nothing of value or worth to offer to this world. We must burn for One Thing only—to know Jesus and glorify His name on the earth no matter what the cost (Psalm 27). We need to willingly embrace a lifestyle of consecration with single-minded focus on the face of Jesus and follow the leadership of the Holy Spirit no matter how uncomfortable it might be (Romans 12:1–2). Healing evangelist Smith Wigglesworth said:

> God wants to flow through you with measureless power of divine utterance and grace till your whole body is a flame of fire. God intends each soul in Pentecost to be a live wire. Not a monument, but a movement. So many people have been baptized with the Holy Ghost; there was a movement but they have become monuments and you cannot move them. God wake us up from out of sleep lest we should become indifferent to the glorious truth and the breath of the Almighty power of God.[2]

When we steward the flame within us, we become conduits for revival fire to flow through us. We no longer remain stagnant but are readily available to move with the Holy Spirit. We become torchbearers who ignite others and set them aflame. Embracing a lifestyle of regular fasting is one way to keep the fire burning.[3] This can help us increase our hunger for more of God and maintain our focus on Jesus' face.

FIREPLACE

Focusing on Jesus in every situation is crucial to our success in being burning ones who don't burn out. The word *focus* comes from a root word that at one time was used to describe fire. In Latin, the word *focus* meant "hearth or fireplace," which figuratively represented "home" and "family."[4] In the dictionary, the word *hearth* means "the floor in front of a fireplace or the lowest part of a furnace where ore or metal is exposed to the flame. It is also used to represent home."[5] Here we see how the word *focus* ties together both the theme of fire and family in one.

In Leviticus 6:9–13, the Lord told Moses to give special instructions to Aaron and his sons that involved making sure there was a consistent fire on the "altar hearth" that never went out. God said through Moses:

> *These are the regulations for the burnt offering: The burnt offering is to remain on the altar* **hearth** *throughout the night, till morning, and the fire must be kept burning on the altar....* **The fire on the altar must be kept burning; it must not go out.** *Every morning the priest is to add firewood and arrange the burnt offering on the fire and burn the fat of the fellowship offerings on it.* **The fire must be kept burning on the altar continuously; it must not go out.**

For the fire of first love to remain in our hearts, it needs to be protected in a safe space. Hearths or fireplaces are specific spaces made for hosting and sustaining fire. A hearth or fireplace can also represent the home or family. Being deeply connected with the family of God is crucial for stewarding revival fire in our hearts, so that it can be sustained and spread to those around us.

QUESTIONS FOR REFLECTION

What does it look like for you to live in the fire of God's presence today? How can you position yourself to live in the fire daily? Is there anything you are holding on to that God might want to burn away from your life to make you more fruitful (John 15)? What does it look like to welcome the fire of God into all areas of your life and fully surrender yourself to the Lord today?

CHAPTER 7

REVIVAL

Wh
hat is revival? And what exactly do we mean when we say that family is the fireplace of revival? Let's add some more context to this phrase and attempt to give a definition for what revival is.

SEMANTICS

Starting with the Scriptures, the term *revive* is used twenty-three times in the Old Testament in the New King James Version. It comes from the Hebrew word הָיָה châyâh, which means "to live, to revive, to keep, leave, or make alive, to give life, quicken, recover, repair, restore to life, save, be whole."[1] Notice the essence is of staying alive once someone has been revived.

The first time the word *revive* is used in the Bible is in Genesis 45:27 when Jacob, who was grieving the loss of his son, realized Joseph was still alive. His spirit revived at that moment.[2] In 1 Kings 17:22, Elijah prayed for a dead child who was brought back to life. Here, the word goes beyond reviving one's hope to mean resurrecting a physical human life.[3] Then in 2 Kings 13:21, a dead body was thrown in Elisha's grave but came back to life when it touched his bones. The word is again used to describe a person who was physically dead returning to life.[4]

The word *revive* is used the most in Psalms (fourteen times), especially throughout Psalm 119. The Psalmist cries out for God to revive him according to His Word, His lovingkindness, His justice, and even His judgments. He also asks God to revive him in His way and in His righteousness. He references turning back to God, deliverance from great troubles, and a hunger to be revived so that God's people may rejoice in Him once again.[5]

In Isaiah, we discover a God who revives the spirit of the humble and the hearts of the contrite ones. In Habakkuk, there is a desire for God to revive and make known His works of old once again.[6] And don't forget the revivals that happened under Kings Asa, Hezekiah, and Josiah, along with many other personal revivals that took place in people's lives throughout Scripture.

In the New Testament, nowhere in the translations do we find the word *revive* or even an equivalent of it. This could be because the Church in the New Testament didn't need revival because they were already living it. Persecution many times proves to help keep people burning hot in their love for Christ.

ETYMOLOGY

When we look deeper into how this word has developed over the centuries, we see that roots for *revive* come from the Old French word *revivre* (10c.) and directly from the Latin word *revivere,* which is translated "to live again." By the 1560s, the word *revive* had the sense of "returning to a flourishing state" or of feelings or activities "beginning to occur again."[7] In the 1650s, *revival* meant the "act of reviving after decline or discontinuance." At the essence of the word *revival* is the call to live again.[8] What has since died and been forgotten needs to be awakened once again.

In the 1660s, there was a unique take on this term. It was used for "the bringing back to the stage of a play which has not been presented for a considerable time."[9] Could it be time for an "encore" on the platform of Christianity, welcoming the Holy Spirit back to take center stage once again? In the early 1700s, it is believed that New England Puritan pastor Cotton Mather was one of the first people to connect this term to religion. In one of his writings in 1702, he linked *revival* with religious awakening in the community.[10] By 1812, the term *revivalist* was used for "one who promotes or leads a religious revival." In 1818, *revival* was used to describe "enthusiastic religious meetings (often by Methodists) meant to inspire revival."[11]

EXPLORING PARADIGMS FOR RELIGIOUS REVIVAL

Moving beyond semantics now into the study of revival history, there are various perspectives on religious revivals by both practitioners and revival historians. For some, revival happens only within the Church, and for others, it is when the world is awakened to Christ as well. Some see revival as something that we should be living in every second of the day, while others see it as episodic moves of God.[12] Some see it coming as a result of prayer, while others see it as a sovereign act of God.

In all my research on revival up to this point (for over two decades now), I have noticed that *hunger* was one of the constants that drew people to seek more of God. This holy desperation regularly resulted in revival. Hunger is a gift from God, something we can pray for. Prayer, surrender, consecration, and repentance many times also preceded personal and corporate revival.

Charles G. Finney (1792–1875), an American Presbyterian minister who was a key leader in the Second Great Awakening and who was also known as the father of modern revivalism, believed that we very much play a role in awakening the Church and in bringing sinners to repentance as God leads. He felt revival needed to happen periodically to wake up the Church because God's people became stagnant so regularly. He saw revival as "nothing else than a new beginning of obedience to God."[13] He compared revival to a crop of wheat and emphasized that God has ways of cultivating both with our partnership. Finney believed that if the fire was kept burning in the Church, there would be no need for revival. Unfortunately, he saw that was rarely the case.[14] About revival he wrote:

> I AM TO SHOW WHAT A REVIVAL IS. It is the renewal of the first love of Christians, resulting in the awakening and conversion of sinners to God. In the popular sense, a revival of religion in a community is the arousing, quickening, and reclaiming of the more or less backslidden church and the more or less general awakening of all classes, and insuring attention to the claims of God.
>
> It presupposes that the church is sunk down in a backslidden state, and a revival consists in the return of a church from her backslidings, and in the conversion of sinners.[15]

Martin Lloyd-Jones (1899–1981), a Welsh-Protestant minister, described revival as "the outpouring of the Spirit over and above his usual, ordinary work; this amazing, unusual, extraordinary thing, which God in his sovereignty and infinite grace has done to the Church from time to time during the long centuries of her history."[16] Christmas Evans (1766–1838), an influential one-eyed Welsh Baptist preacher, said, "Revival is God bending down to the dying embers of a fire that is just about to go out, and breathing into it, until it bursts again into flame." South African pastor Andrew Murray (1828-1917) who helped transform the Church to become more missional said, "A true revival means nothing less than a revolution, casting out the spirit of worldliness, making God's love triumph in the heart."[17] Duncan Campbell (1898-1972), a Scottish evangelist who played a significant role in the Hebrides Revival (or Lewis Awakening) said that "Revival is a community saturated with God."[18]

In his study on Pentecostalism in *The Everlasting Gospel*, William Faupel sees revival as having a seven-stage process: conception, gestation, labor, birth, growth, reproduction, and maturity.[19] He compares it to the life cycle of a new baby. Mark Stibbe from the UK defines revival as "a season ordained by God in which the Holy Spirit awakens the Church to evangelise the lost, and the lost to their dire need of Jesus Christ."[20] He distinguishes renewal as confined to the Church, while revival reaches beyond the Church and into the world.[21] He likens renewal to a stream and revival to that same river becoming a "flood that disturbs boulders and overflows banks."[22] Like Stibbe, I would also say there are unique seasons, windows of opportunity, or *kairos* moments where the Spirit is at work to awaken and revive the Church in a special way.[23]

DEFINING REVIVAL

Revival is when the fire of first love for Jesus is reignited in the hearts of believers. As a result, their lives are transformed, and the kingdom of God is expanded all around them in various ways that impact, shape, and reform culture and society.

Revival is for Christians whose fire has waned. If someone has never encountered God's love for themselves, they can't necessarily be reawakened to it. It is only when the fire of first love has been snuffed out that one needs revival. Once that original flame is reignited, the awakened ones naturally influence those around them, and many times others are brought to salvation as a result.

Ultimately, revival is becoming fully alive to Jesus again. And it's important to understand that revival is not the end goal. It is only just the beginning.

QUESTIONS FOR REFLECTION

What was your previous understanding of revival? After reading this chapter, has anything changed? How would you define revival now?

CHAPTER 8

JUST THE BEGINNING

In the natural, if someone is sleeping, barely alive, or has suddenly died, they need to be awakened or *revived*. Depending on the situation, one might use smelling salts (ammonia inhalants) to awaken someone who has passed out. The stimulating salts are placed under the person's nose. When they breathe in, they are suddenly revived from their previous unconscious state. At this point, it is futile to continue to give them smelling salts or attempt to wake them up. They have already come back to life. This person must now begin to *live* a more empowered life since their awakening.

This can be a metaphor for revival. Some people have become spiritually unconscious or fallen asleep, and they need to be reawakened. Others have become "dead" inside and need to be resurrected. However, once they have awakened, it's then time to move from the just-resurrected state to the empowered state of living, being transformed, and stepping into their destiny.

Revival is only just the beginning. Once a person is awakened, then it's time to fully *live*. Hosea 6:2 says, "After two days He will *revive* us; on the third day He will raise us up, that we may *live* in His sight" (NKJV). Here we see that revival is not meant to be a continual state as much as what needs to happen whenever our spirits begin to wither away or die on the inside. Once people are revived, they then need to *live* the abundant life Jesus died for them to have (John 10:10). Transformation, reformation, revolution, and destiny must follow. Once revived, they need to learn how to live as burning ones on fire for Jesus, constantly remaining full of the oil of His presence.

JESUS IS REVIVAL

All that being said, at the heart of revival is Jesus. Jesus is the truest revival we will ever know. Beyond living for revival, we live for the Reviver. When we become awakened spiritually, we fall more in love with Jesus. When we fall more in love with Jesus, transformation takes place within our hearts, and we impact those around us. Revival is truly just more of Jesus.

We were born to live revived lives in the Spirit of God. We were made to be burning ones who don't burn out. We are here to live loudly for the King of kings and display His glory through our lives. As we become awakened to King Jesus, our destinies begin to unfold in a greater measure. We step out in faith, hand in hand with our best friend, Jesus, and can bring hope to a world that desperately needs it. From a place of intimate union with God, as we yield to and follow the Holy Spirit's leading, we become agents of revival wherever we go. The burning flame inside spreads, and it begins to ignite others whose flames have dwindled.

THE REVIVER

Rolland Baker, co-founder with his wife Heidi Baker of Iris Global, is a missionary in Mozambique who has experienced revival firsthand. His insights in the epilogue of his book *Keeping the Fire* are worth noting here.

I return at the end to where I began: with the Person of Jesus.

Iris is not about us. It is about *Jesus*.

Revival is not about manifestations or miracles; it is about the Reviver, Jesus our Savior.

We have only one destination, one home, one reality, one resting place, one source, one motivation, one reward, one possession, one point of contact with God, one source of real satisfaction—and that is Jesus....

Everything we value has been found in Jesus. The key to our core values is therefore falling in love with Him.

Love is a gift of relationship, not just self-sacrifice. The secret place is not necessarily found in a prayer closet or a posture of soaking, or in battling for a just cause, or in a massive prayer and fasting effort. Even the most amazing miracles can leave us lonely and without relationship. We can run out of motivation advancing the noblest ideals and working at all levels to transform society. We can minister until we have no more strength, and still go home and lie in bed without the relationship for which our hearts are made.

Everything is okay with relationship. It is all that Jesus cares about, all that motivates Him. He could do many more amazing miracles to dazzle the world with His powers, but He is interested only in relationship. The entire creation, all the grandeur of the physical world, and all His works are designed to serve one thing: *relationship*. Revival has no content without it. Renewal and manifestations are pointless apart from it. Miracles only find their meaning in it. Joy is shallow and groundless unless rooted in it. Without relationship we are the living dead ....

Revival is all about Jesus.[1]

REVIVAL WITHOUT GOD

Revival can easily become an idol in our lives and take the place of Jesus. It can possess us and become an obsession. Not that there's anything wrong with desiring revival, but if anything comes before our passionate pursuit of Jesus, it becomes idolatry. We always need to seek Jesus first, yield to the Holy Spirit, and pursue the God of revival. Revival should never become an idol in our lives. Our obsession above all else, including revival, must remain loving Jesus wholeheartedly. As we love God with all our minds, hearts, bodies, and spirits, revival is a natural overflow.

We don't want to end up one day in front of God sharing how we released "revival" in the world but did it apart from personal and intimate relationship with Him. What would be the point of doing signs and wonders without Him or without love (1 Corinthians 13)? Moses could have easily seen revival, stepped into his destiny, and watched his dreams come true. But without God's presence, he wasn't going to move (Exodus 33).

Revival without Jesus is not only empty, it is dangerous. Jesus says in Matthew 7:21–23:

> *Not everyone who says to me, "Lord, Lord," will enter the kingdom of heaven, but only the one who does the will of my Father who is in heaven. Many will say to me on that day, "Lord, Lord, did we not prophesy in your name and in your name drive out demons and in your name perform many miracles?"*

Then I will tell them plainly, "I never knew you. Away from me, you evildoers!"

Casting out demons, setting the oppressed free, and performing miracles definitely *feel like* revival and that the kingdom of God has come in people's lives. The only problem is that doing any of these works of revival is dangerous when not deeply connected to the Source of revival, which is Jesus Himself. It appears from this passage that it is quite possible to do the works of revival without being known by God. This is unsafe ground to walk on. We must do the Father's will *and* remain connected in relationship with Jesus as we do the works of revival. In their book *A God-Sized Vision: Revival Stories that Stretch and Stir,* Hansen and Woodbridge say, "You can have signs and wonders, but if you don't have God, you don't have revival. God-centered revivals withstand the temptation to treasure the blessings of revival over the one who blesses."[2]

More than anything, revival needs to be birthed from a place of deep, burning passion for God and from an overflowing relationship with Him. As we stay connected to the Source, His steadily burning and increasing flame within us will ignite and awaken many around us, releasing revival wherever we go. As we knit ourselves to other burning ones and learn how to live in the fire of His presence together, we encounter His love and power in a way that radically impacts our world.

As we long for revival fire to be ignited in our own hearts and for those flames to spread to a lost and dying world, we must also remember to honor the sacrifices of those who came before us. We must follow in their footsteps to pave the way for future generations of revivalists to follow behind us.

QUESTIONS FOR REFLECTION

What have your experiences with revival been like so far? Do you know someone who carries and releases revival well? What are some character-istics about that person that inspire you? What core value do you want to shape your perspective of revival?

CHAPTER 9

WAITING FOR
THE FIRE

A good example of family as the fireplace of revival was lived out over two thousand years ago when a community of believers gathered around the presence of God, waiting for the fire. When the Pentecostal fire from on high fell upon them in a *kairos* moment, these fearful believers were transformed and radically emboldened. But first they had to wait for it. Together.

FIRST THINGS FIRST

Shortly before disappearing from this earth and while sharing a meal with His disciples, Jesus said, "Do not leave Jerusalem, but wait for the gift my Father promised, which you have heard me speak about. For John baptized with water, but in a few days you will be baptized with the Holy Spirit" (Acts 1:4–5). Jesus' friends and followers were told to do one of the hardest things most of us will ever have to do in our lifetimes—*wait*.

Wait.

That four-letter word that stirs up an intense internal struggle within all of us. *Wait* for the gift of the Spirit. Anticipation. Expectation. They knew something was coming; they could feel it in their bones. But they had no idea *when* this promise would be fulfilled. So, they had to wait. Together. In this impending *kairos* moment.

The Greek word used for *wait* in this passage is *perimenō*. One of the two Greek words that make up this word is *menō*, which means "to abide." It can also mean "to remain, dwell, tarry, stand, endure, or to continue to be present."[1] There is something active about the waiting here. It is standing against any resistance that might come. It is enduring the temptation to wander away from community or the word of the Lord. One must fight a war to remain present in the midst of an anxious world (Psalm 27). But that is what Jesus called His friends to do. They were to wait for the gift from the Father together (Luke 24:49). With great anticipation, they knew that something very special was coming to them, for He had also said in Acts 1:8, "But you will receive power when the Holy Spirit comes upon you; and you will be my witnesses in Jerusalem and in all Judea and Samaria, and to the ends of the earth."

Following Jesus' direction, His friends returned to Jerusalem and gathered in the upper room. There, "they all joined together constantly in prayer along with the women and Mary the mother of Jesus, with his brothers" (Acts 1:14).

Then, not many days later, everything changed. They stepped into the momentum of heaven together. As they were waiting upon the Lord, the promise of the Father was released to them.

> *When the day of Pentecost came, they were all together in one place. Suddenly a sound like the blowing of a violent wind came from heaven and filled the whole house where they were sitting. They saw what seemed to be tongues of fire that separated and came to rest on each of them. All of them were filled with the Holy Spirit and began to speak in other tongues as the Spirit enabled them.*
>
> Acts 2:1–4

INAUGURATION OF A NEW ERA

As this family of believers waited upon the Lord, the fire of God rested upon them, and they were all filled with the Holy Spirit. They were marked by this radical gift of God's presence filling their very beings. New languages overflowed as a result of this Pentecostal fire that was released. This was an inauguration into a new era.

Many in the city were drawn to this commotion. They could feel the power of God that had descended. Most did not understand and were confused. But then Peter stood up and preached boldly to the crowds, and "those who accepted his message were baptized, and about three thousand were added to their number that day" (Acts 2:41).

After the fire fell from heaven, three thousand people were converted in one day! Instant revival happened. Regardless of how many people your church currently has, can you imagine what would happen if three thousand believers were added to your number overnight?! That would blow apart every preexisting structure and plan. It would force the need for a new wineskin.

The new believers' hunger was apparent, and the early Church responded to this massive influx of new converts. In Acts 2:42–47, Luke says that the new converts:

> *Devoted themselves to the apostles' teaching and to fellowship, to the breaking of bread and to prayer. Everyone was filled with awe at the many wonders and signs performed by the apostles. All the believers were together and had everything in common. They sold property and possessions to give to anyone who had need. Every day they continued to meet together in the temple courts. They broke bread in their homes and ate together with glad and sincere hearts, praising God and enjoying the favor of all the people. And the Lord added to their number daily those who were being saved.*

Acts provides us with a paradigm for how to sustain the fires of revival. These believers chose to steward this move of God by cultivating healthy community and discipleship within the body of Christ. The apostles were faithful to teach, equip, and provide a family for the newly converted believers.

The word used for *fellowship* in the New Testament is *koinonia*, which can mean "community, communion, joint participation, communication, contribution, and distribution."[2] The believers shared everything they had and made sure those in need were taken care of. *Every* day they met together in the temple, *and* they also regularly shared meals in each other's homes, praising God. They gathered around the table together to fellowship with one another. This community became the fireplace of revival so that the flames of Pentecost would not wither.

A little later in Acts 5, Peter and the other apostles were imprisoned, beaten, and told to be silent for their faith. They left that time of persecution rejoicing for being found worthy to co-suffer for the sake of Christ. Right after this, Acts 5:42 says, "And daily in the temple, *and* in every house, they did not cease teaching and preaching Jesus as the Christ" (NKJV).

The apostles in the book of Acts gathered in the temple, or what we might call church, to proclaim the gospel, *and* they also met in private homes to disciple the new converts. They realized the importance of meeting together in the wider corporate meetings to teach the truth and share vision *and* also saw significance in nurturing the newer believers in the smaller setting of a home. The rhythm of the Christian life in the early Church was not *either* larger gatherings *or* smaller house meetings. Both the larger public gatherings *and* the smaller, more intimate home settings played a role in staying connected during this move of God.

The existing believers took ownership to enfold the new believers into the family of God and even into their own homes. As these were intentional to steward the flame of revival, welcome the incoming harvest of souls, seek God, and grow in their faith together, the Lord added many who were being saved. When the family of God truly loves each other, it's attractive to those who don't yet know Him as their Father. The world is looking for a place they can call *home*. They are searching for a tribe, or spiritual family, that will love and accept them for who they are. They are longing to be a part of a family and searching for a place to belong before they become believers. And when they discover the family of God truly loving each other well, of course they will want to dive right in.

The early believers chose to come together and wait in unity for the promise of the Lord to be fulfilled, and God crashed in upon them. Many people were saved when a group of hungry believers gathered to seek more of God. They knew that they didn't have the capacity or strength to steward revival alone. These early believers knew the significance of being knit together as the body of Christ. They realized that they needed each other. This family of believers became a fireplace for stewarding revival. And because they came together in unity as one, revival spread like wildfire.

QUESTIONS FOR REFLECTION

Have you been baptized in the Holy Spirit and fire? If not, what does it look like to seek God in this way? If you have, what does it look like to position yourself for a fresh baptism of the Holy Spirit and fire and to ask God to increase the presence of His Holy Spirit upon your life? Who do you know who would love to gather around the table of fellowship and God's presence to seek more of His glory and fire with you?

PART 3

MORAVIAN LEGACY

Before diving into the following story, I want to warn you—whenever I share about the Moravians, God always does something powerful.

When I shared about the Moravians with the Destiny House community I led while living in Redding, California, during one of our family nights, God took us into a deep encounter with Him. This led into a time of spontaneous worship where we lingered together in His presence, and many experienced the Father's healing love in a significant way. As we worshiped and waited on the Holy Spirit, one person began to repent and confess her sins; another began to weep and receive deep healing. We soaked in His presence into the late hours of the night, feasting on God together as family in the upper room. All of this happened after sharing the testimony of the Moravians.

Another time, I shared the story of the Moravians at a ministry school in Germany, and the fire of God fell on us so powerfully that both of my translators fell out in the Spirit, and I had to get a third one. After I had finished teaching, the students gathered in one big circle and declared what they were born for. As they vulnerably stepped out to share their hearts, the fire of God descended again and marked them with power.[1]

I encourage you to open wide your heart and read the following pages with great expectation. Let the Moravians' testimony prophesy over you (Revelation 19:10). May the soil of your heart be ready to receive the seeds of testimony that are about to be planted. As you learn more about how God moved within the Moravian community to shape history, may a fresh fire be ignited within you.

CHAPTER 10

THE INVISIBLE BODY

It is remarkable how one act of hospitality in providing a home for a refugee impacted Christianity as we know it today. I doubt that Count Nikolaus von Zinzendorf had any idea of the ripple effects his one "yes" would have on future generations.

Nikolaus von Zinzendorf (May 26, 1700–May 9, 1760) originally from Dresden, Germany, grew up in a wealthy Christian home. When he was only six weeks old, his father died suddenly of a burst blood vessel. Just before he died, he took Nikolaus in his arms and consecrated him to "the service of Christ."[1] Little did his father realize how this one holy act would mark his son for the rest of his life.

When Zinzendorf was still a young child, his grandmother took him in to care for him at Gross-Hennersdorf Castle, where he grew up around devout Pietist Christians. Even at a young age, his thirst to know God was apparent as he began reading the Bible every day. Looking back, he remembered that "already in my childhood, I loved the Saviour, and had abundant communion with Him. In my fourth year I began to seek God earnestly, and determined to become a true servant of Jesus Christ." When he was six, he "regarded Christ as his Brother, and would talk with Him for hours together as with a familiar friend and was often found rapt in thought, like Socrates in the market-place at Athens."[2] When he was ten years old, his mother took him to a school in Halle.

Whenever he had breaks from his studies and returned to the castle, he would overhear Pietist leaders speaking about "Churches within the Church" that had been established in several noble Lutheran families.[3] He longed to have a community like that for himself, so he decided to form several religious societies at his school. He started a society for boys that was first called a "Church within the Church," then changed to "The Slaves of Virtue," next the "Confessors of Christ," until finally they became known as the "Honourable Order of the Mustard Seed." As the boys grew into men, many notable people joined their ranks, including archbishops, bishops, and governors. Their emblem was a small shield with the motto "His wounds our healing." Further, each member "wore a gold ring, inscribed with the words, 'No man liveth unto himself.'" [4] They were committed in covenantal love to build each other up in Christ.

Zinzendorf was later sent off to the University of Wittenberg to study law, just in time for the two-hundred-year anniversary of Martin Luther's Protestant Reformation that was ignited there. While there, "he studied the Bible in Hebrew and Greek, spent whole nights in prayer, fasted the livelong day on Sundays," and reached out to the theology professors to connect deeper on matters about God.[5] Following his time in Wittenberg, he did a traveling tour and went to Paris. There he became friends with the Catholic Archbishop who tried to have him join the Church of Rome. Zinzendorf chose not to join because he believed the Church existed in many forms. J. E. Hutton, historian of the Moravian movement, said that Zinzendorf:

> Came to the conclusion that the true Church of Jesus Christ consisted of many sects and many forms of belief. He held that the Church was still an invisible body; he held that it transcended the bounds of all denominations; he had found good Christians among Protestants and Catholics alike; and he believed with all his heart and

soul, that God had called him to the holy task of enlisting the faithful in all the sects in one grand Christian army, and thus realizing, in visible form, the promise of Christ that all His disciples should be one. He was no bigoted Lutheran. For him the cloak of creed or sect was only of minor moment. He desired to break down all sectarian barriers. He desired to draw men from all the churches into one grand fellowship with Christ.[6]

Zinzendorf desired to enlist the faithful "in one grand Christian army" regardless of class, affiliation, or denominational barrier. Even from a young age, he had his heart set on the unity of the saints and bringing the "invisible body" together as one.

SURRENDERING LOVE

In 1720, near the end of his tour, Zinzendorf stopped by to see his aunt, the Countess of Castell. He got sick and had to extend his stay there. During this time, sparks of love for his cousin Theodora emerged, with the approval of the family to pursue her. However, when he consulted his friend Count Reuss, he discovered that he also had intentions to pursue Theodora. They both deferred to the other and encouraged the other to court her. Zinzendorf believed that if his love for her was pure, then he could as easily hand her over to be loved by his friend. Finally, since they were getting nowhere in their resolution, they decided to ask Theodora who she would choose. She readily chose to give her hand in marriage to Count Reuss.

Even with a broken heart, Zinzendorf trusted God with this surrender. He composed a song to be sung at their wedding and released a prayer that moved people to tears at the ceremony. About eighteen months later, Zinzendorf found his bride-to-be, and it just happened to be Count Reuss' sister. On September 7, 1722, he married Erdmuth Dorothea, whom the Moravians would later call the "foster-mother of the Brethren's Church in the eighteenth century."[7]

DIVINE CONNECTION

Longing to bring the gospel beyond the nobles and elite to poor peasants, Zinzendorf purchased the little estate of Berthelsdorf in Herrnhut, Germany. He appointed his friend John Andrew Rothe to be a pastor of a village church there. Zinzendorf deeply desired to give his life for the poor and to win many souls of all different classes for Christ.

In 1722, Zinzendorf had a divine connection that would change the trajectory of his life. He met a man named Christian David who was fleeing the religious persecution in his home of Moravia (now present-day Czech Republic) to seek a safer life in Germany. When Christian David arrived in Germany, he approached Zinzendorf to ask if he could settle on his estate. Little did Zinzendorf know at the time that this refugee carried a key to his own destiny. Thankfully, Zinzendorf eventually welcomed him to find asylum and settle on his land. In this one act of kindness, an exchange of gifts took place that went beyond what either of them could have imagined.

Through Zinzendorf's hospitality, Christian David saw hope for his people. Recognizing the favor he had with Zinzendorf, he went back to his homeland and began to rescue others who were being persecuted because of the Protestant Reformation. He invited them, too, to settle in Herrnhut. Zinzendorf was generous in making space for these refugees on the land God had entrusted him with. He was also fascinated by their Christian beliefs and the way they shared all things in common. Even though Zinzendorf was a man of royalty, he recognized there was something in these people he needed. Because he was so drawn to the community of refugees and captivated by their communal way of life, he decided to move on-site to live with them in Herrnhut.

QUESTIONS FOR REFLECTION

What stood out to you the most about Zinzendorf's life so far and why? What does a "church within a church" look like to you? Have you had any divine connections? What would it look like to invite the Holy Spirit to reveal more of God's purposes for these special connections?

CHAPTER 11

MORAVIAN PENTECOST

Zinzendorf had a vision to steward his land and the people God brought to him. With only the Bible as his source, his initial purpose was ecumenical in nature. He wanted to unify the churches into a single Lutheran community with "little churches within a church." But in the process of building this community, he said, "I acknowledge no Christianity without fellowship."[1] He discovered that within the Moravian people were ancient wells of the Brethren Church.

In July 1727, he found a work by John Amos Comenius, a Czech theologian known as the father of modern education. While reading Comenius' Latin version of the old Brethren's "Account of Discipline," Zinzendorf had an awakening, which Hutton recounts this way:

> As the Count devoured the ancient treatise, he noticed that the rules laid down therein were almost the same as the rules which he had just drawn up for the refugees at Herrnhut. He returned to Herrnhut, reported his find, and read the good people extracts from the book {Aug. 4th.}. The sensation was profound. If this was like new milk to the Count it was like old wine to the Brethren; and again the fire of their fathers burned in their veins.[2]

When he made this discovery, his eyes were opened. He realized he didn't need to make this community fit into a certain mold. There was already a supernatural synergy taking place. God was intersecting streams of heritage and bringing together deep wells. God had knit these kindred-spirits together for a greater purpose than any had originally imagined.

A FIRE IS IGNITED

We all know that when there is community living closely together, there is room for disagreement and conflict. It was no different with this group of refugees. In 1727, there began to be great contention among the Moravians. Because this went sharply against Zinzendorf's heart for unity, he determined that something needed to change. The leadership of the community decided to write out common values they wanted to share as a Christian community. They set aside August 13, 1727, as the day they would come together at the chapel in Berthelsdorf to consecrate their lives unto the Lord and covenant with each other.

> The date fixed was Monday, August 13th [1727]. The sense of awe was overpowering. As the Brethren walked down the slope to the church all felt that the supreme occasion had arrived; and all who had quarrelled [sic] in the days gone by made a covenant of loyalty and love. At the door of the church the strange sense of awe was thrilling.
>
> They entered the building; the service began; the "Confession" was offered by the Count [Zinzendorf]; and then, at one and the same moment, all present, rapt in deep devotion, were stirred by the mystic wondrous touch of a power which none could define or understand.

There, in Berthelsdorf Parish Church, they attained at last the firm conviction that they were one in Christ; and there, above all, they believed and felt that on them, as on the twelve disciples on the Day of Pentecost, had rested the purifying fire of the Holy Ghost.

"We learned," said the Brethren, "to love." "From that time onward," said David Nitschmann, "Herrnhut was a living Church of Jesus Christ."[3]

As they put aside their differences to come together as one, choosing to make a covenant of love with one another, the power of God and the purifying fire of the Holy Ghost fell upon them. Revival had come. Contending for unity proved catalytic to ignite this flame. Where the enemy wanted to stir up strife, contention, and discord in this community born for unity, they answered back with a resolute firmness to stand against all his divisive schemes. They knew their destiny was unity and love. After that moment, what tried to divide them brought them closer together. This event later became known as the Moravian Pentecost.

STEWARDING THE FIRE THROUGH THE FURNACE OF PRAYER

Now that they had the fire, they realized they would need to steward it so they wouldn't lose it. On August 27, 1727, just two weeks after the ancient outpouring of love, a small group within the Moravian community arranged "a system of Hourly Intercession," so this blessing would not be lost.[4] Thus, the seeds for a one-hundred-year prayer meeting were planted. Hutton writes:

As the fire on the altar in the Jewish Temple was never allowed to go out, so the Brethren resolved that in this new temple of the Lord the incense of intercessory prayer should rise continually day and night. Henceforth, Herrnhut in very truth should be the 'Watch of the Lord.' The whole day was carefully mapped out, and each Brother or Sister took his or her turn. Of all the prayer unions ever organized surely this was one of the most remarkable. It is said to have lasted without interruption for over a hundred years.[5]

The people had an allotted time when they would pray no matter what they were doing. They didn't stop their work to go into the prayer closet in the middle of the day during their assigned hour of prayer. Instead, they continued in their normal work and interceded at the same time. In response to their conviction for unity and the powerful outpouring of the Holy Spirit that followed, the Protestant 24/7 Prayer Movement was birthed that lasted uninterrupted for one hundred years.

One of the greatest weaknesses within the Moravian community of disunity, turned around to become one of their greatest strengths of unity in love. I wonder what God might want to birth today within our generation when we all come together, lay down our armor, and seek to worship Jesus in unity as family.

BURNING ONES

These Moravians were burning ones who wanted their lives to be the altar where the fire never went out. There was a high call for consecration in their community. They wanted to be holy, fully set apart, and pleasing to God no matter the cost. Even some of the women went to extremes so that they could live fully devoted to Jesus without any distractions.

Hutton describes a promise some of the women made together on May 4, 1730:

> The single young women, led by Anna Nitschmann, agreed to live in a "Single Sister's House," and made a covenant with one another that henceforth they would not make matrimony the highest aim in life, but would rather, like Mary of Bethany, sit at the feet of Christ and learn of Him.[6]

These Moravians wanted their fire for the Lord to be kept burning on the altar continually, as Leviticus 6:8–13 describes. They modeled what it looks like to become living sacrifices (Romans 12:1–2). They were all in for Jesus. God was preparing them in the furnace of intercession to pay the ultimate price of laying down their lives for the sake of the gospel.

QUESTIONS FOR REFLECTION

What does it look like to lay your life on the altar, where God's fire remains burning day and night, not just on a Sunday morning at church? What does it look like to lay down your armor, agendas, and offenses and choose to love and honor the person in front of you today? What might God want to birth and release through your life when you reconcile with the one He is highlighting to you? What is the role of unity in relation to revival? Why is unity so important for stewarding God's fire and glory?

CHAPTER 12

RADICAL MISSIONS

After their covenantal prayer movement began, Zinzendorf had another unique divine appointment that would again shift the trajectory of this community of refugees. When he went to Denmark for a coronation of a new king in 1731, he met a Christian slave named Anthony Ulrich from St. Thomas in the West Indies.[1] Anthony shared with him how there was a huge need to bring the gospel to the slaves there. His pleas struck a chord with Zinzendorf. When he returned from his trip, even though it was 2:00 a.m., he noticed a light was on in the house where the single brethren lived. He went straight there to find them all on "their knees in prayer."[2] He then shared the news of what he had experienced.

Zinzendorf was deeply moved by Anthony's stories and later invited him to come share with his community in Herrnhut. Anthony said that "no one could be a missionary in St. Thomas without first becoming a slave."[3] Zinzendorf was burdened for these slaves to know Jesus. The Moravians were also lit on fire to help these people.

More than a year after meeting Anthony, and after much prayer and preparation, this unified community decided to send two young men who were willing to sell themselves into slavery to be tortured, tormented, and persecuted, so they could win the other slaves to Jesus. On August 21, 1732, after spending the whole night in prayer, Zinzendorf drove Leonard Dober and David Nitschmann fifteen miles to drop them off near the harbor with only thirty shillings to their names. Filled with faith, they ended up getting on a ship headed to St. Thomas.[4] When they arrived there, they sold themselves into slavery to reach the slaves for Jesus.

This one radical act of obedience paved the way for the Protestant modern mission's movement. Hutton recognizes:

> They were the founders of Christian work among the slaves. For fifty years the Moravian Brethren laboured in the West Indies without any aid from any other religious denomination. They established churches in St. Thomas, in St. Croix, in St. John's, in Jamaica, in Antigua, in Barbados, and in St. Kitts. They had 13,000 baptized converts before a missionary from any other Church arrived on the scene.[5]

Not long after these two pioneered missions in the West Indies, another pair of Moravian missionaries were sent to Greenland to minister to the Eskimos. They learned their language and served the people there. Then, others were sent to Africa, Asia, and other places around the world. Whenever a message came back to Herrnhut that two, five, or twelve had died, the same number—or often double that number—would volunteer to replace the martyrs on their battlefield.

A furnace of intercession at home covered those out in the field. They remained connected, shielded, and united in prayer. In this way, the whole community was able to participate in what God was doing in other regions.[6]

LIVING INCARNATIONALLY

When these Moravians went to other mission fields, they chose to live incarnationally with the people. They didn't go to a new place acting superior to the nationals they were trying to reach. They didn't try to colonize, indoctrinate, or enculturate the people to make them live the way they did. Instead, they humbled themselves, went low, learned the language, and sought to understand and relate to the people where they were at. They brought God to the people and allowed the Holy Spirit to bring the transformation. They went as servants. Their posture of stepping onto the mission field is something we can all learn from. Their example of going low and even being willing to lose their lives for the sake of the gospel is both inspiring and convicting.

QUESTIONS FOR REFLECTION

What stood out the most to you about the Moravians in relation to missions and why? What does it look like for you to be a laid-down lover in your everyday life at home or at work?

CHAPTER 13

PEACE IN THE STORM

In October 1735, three years after Dober and Nitschmann catalyzed a powerful mission's movement, other missionaries replaced them on St. Thomas Island so they could continue to do more pioneering missions. This time, they set sail to bring the gospel to North America. A few months into their journey by boat, a dangerous storm arose. The Moravians began to worship Jesus in the midst of the storm. Other missionaries on the ship were struck by their faith. They couldn't believe how calm they were in the face of what seemed to be impending death.

There was one English missionary on board who feared for his life and was not even certain of his salvation in that moment. John Wesley (1703–1791) wrote in his journal on January 25, 1736:

> At noon our third storm began. At four it was more violent than before.... At seven I went to the Germans [Moravian missionaries]. I had long before observed the great seriousness of their behaviour. Of their humility they had given a continual proof, by performing those servile offices for other passengers, which none of the English would undertake; for which they desired, and would receive no pay, saying, "it was good for their proud hearts," and "their loving Saviour had done more for them." And every day had given them occasion of showing meekness,

which no injury could move. If they were pushed, struck, or thrown down, they rose and again and went away; but no complaint was found in their mouth. There was now an opportunity of trying, whether they were delivered from the spirit of fear, as well as from that of pride, anger, and revenge.

In the midst of the psalm wherewith their service began, the sea broke over, split the mainsail in pieces, covered the ship, and poured in between the decks, as if the great deep had already swallowed us up. A terrible screaming began among the English. The Germans calmly sung on. I asked one of them afterwards, "Was you not afraid?" He answered, "I thank God, no." I asked, "But were not your women and children afraid?" He replied, mildly, "No; our women and children are not afraid to die."

From them I went to their crying, trembling neighbours, and pointed out to them the difference in the hour of trial, between him that feareth God, and him that feareth him not.[1]

When Wesley saw the Moravians worshiping in the storm, he was struck to the core by the peace and surety these missionaries had. He recognized they had something he needed.

Making it through the storm in one piece, Wesley became increasingly drawn to the Moravians to learn more about their deep-rooted and unshakable faith in Jesus. On February 6, 1736, they arrived safely and "first set foot on American soil."[2] The very next day, Wesley had the opportunity to converse with Mr. Spangenberg, one of the "Pastors of the Germans" (or Moravian missionaries). Wesley recalled:

I soon found what spirit he was of; and asked his advice with regard to my own conduct. He said, "My brother, I must first ask you one of two questions. Have you the witness within yourself? Does the Spirit of God bear witness with your spirit, that you are a child of God?" I was surprised, and knew not what to answer. He observed it and asked, "Do you know Jesus Christ?" I paused, and said, "I know he is the Saviour of the world." "True," replied he; "but do you know he saved you?" I answered, "I hope he has died to save me." He only added, "Do you know yourself?" I said, "I do." But I fear they were vain words.[3]

That was where John Wesley was in his faith journey as he approached his thirty-third birthday. He was a missionary who had given his life to help bring others to salvation, yet he wasn't even sure if he was saved. He had religion and some theology, but these things were outside of a secure personal relationship. He was trying to apply an impersonal faith to a personal God. He realized by observing the character of these Moravian missionaries that they had a different level of faith than he had. He knew something needed to change.

He began to converse with them more often, and they taught him what it meant to have full assurance of salvation. He watched the way they lived in meekness and humility and was moved. He had many theological discussions with them to learn more about their radical trust in God. On Tuesday, February 24, 1736, Wesley mentioned in his journal that he had connected with Nitschmann and Dober. Wesley and these missionaries were in Savannah at the same time to look for land to build a house on. The following night because of a delay, Wesley and a friend "took up lodging with the Germans."[4] Getting an up-close look at the personal life of these Moravian missionaries, he said:

We had now an opportunity, day by day, of observing their whole behaviour. For we were in one room with them from morning to night, unless for the little time I spent in walking. They were always employed, always cheerful themselves, and in good humour with one another; they had put away all anger, and strife, and wrath, and bitterness, and clamour, and evil-speaking; they walked worthy of the vocation wherewith they were called, and adorned the Gospel of our Lord in all things.[5]

The Moravians' covenant for unity continued to bear fruit right before Wesley's eyes. After a challenging mission to the Native Americans in Georgia, wrought with personal heartbreak, a lawsuit against him, and with his head hung low, Wesley headed back to his homeland full of self-doubt on December 22, 1737. Thankfully, God prepared another divine intersection for Wesley in London. There, on February 7, 1738, he met a Moravian missionary named Peter Böhler who had recently been ordained by Zinzendorf.[6] They spent much time together conversing over spiritual matters, which stirred Wesley.

STRANGELY WARMED (MAY 24, 1738)

A couple of months later, some of Wesley's friends invited him to go to a meeting on Aldersgate Street. The preacher was reading a preface to the commentary of Romans written by Martin Luther. As Wesley was listening to this, his heart was strangely warmed by the fire of God. He recounted:

About a quarter before nine, while he was describing the change which God works in the heart through faith in

Christ, I felt my heart strangely warmed. I felt I did trust in Christ, Christ alone, for salvation; and an assurance was given me that He had taken away my sins, even mine, and saved me from the law of sin and death. I began to pray with all my might for those who had in a more especial manner despitefully used me and persecuted me. I then testified openly to all there what I now first felt in my heart.[7]

Wesley finally experienced God's love and fire for himself. His faith came alive. He stepped into and received his personal encounter with the living God. He was marked in such a profound way that everything shifted in his life from that point forward.

Never underestimate the power of your decision to worship Jesus in every storm of life. People are watching. Who knows if the next reformer is waiting to be catalyzed as they observe your resolve to fix your eyes upon Jesus and worship Him in every storm.

QUESTIONS FOR REFLECTION

How can you posture your heart today to worship Jesus in the midst of the storms of life? Is there anyone you know who stewards radical peace? What could it look like to spend more time learning from them?

CHAPTER 14

RIPPLE EFFECTS

Less than two months after his life-changing defining moment, Wesley headed to Germany to learn more about the way of life of the Moravians who had impacted him so greatly. On June 7, 1738, Wesley wrote in his journal about his longing to spend more time receiving from the Moravians:

> I determined, if God should permit, to retire for a short time into Germany. I had fully proposed, before I left Georgia, so to do, if it should please God to bring me back to Europe. And I now clearly saw the time was come. My weak mind could not bear to be thus sawn asunder. And I hoped the conversing with those holy men who were themselves living witnesses of the full power of faith, and yet able to bear with those that are weak, would be a means, under God, of so establishing my soul, that I might go from faith to faith, and from "strength to strength."[1]

While Wesley was in Herrnhut, he got to meet Zinzendorf as well as Christian David and many more key leaders in the movement. He spent three months there before returning to England.

The Moravians provided the atmosphere, community, and experience to help "midwife" Wesley into his destiny. Shortly after his return to England, Wesley participated in a love feast gathering on New Year's Eve that would have ripple effects for centuries to come.

GREAT AWAKENING (JANUARY 1, 1739)

On January 1, 1739, in the early morning hours before the sun came up, John Wesley was with his brother and friends worshiping into the new year. Suddenly, God's power fell mightily upon the group. Wesley recalled in his journal:

> Mon. Jan. 1, 1739. Mr. Hall, Kinchin, Ingham, White-field, Hutchins, and my brother Charles, were present at our love-feast in Fetter-lane, with about sixty of our brethren. About three in the morning, as we were continuing instant in prayer, the power of God came mightily upon us, insomuch that many cried out for exceeding joy, and many fell to the ground. As soon as we were recovered a little from that awe and amazement at the presence of his Majesty, we broke out with one voice, "We praise thee, O God, we acknowledge thee to be the Lord."[2]

This meeting marked the beginning of the Great Awakening. Immediately following this, Wesley began to open air preach. Many got saved. Great and unusual signs and wonders began to break out. He went on to establish the Methodist Movement, where he raised up and released untrained laypeople to do the works of the kingdom of God. He rode over 250,000 miles on horseback, preached over 40,000 sermons, and published over 5,000 books. By 1830, Methodism was the largest denomination in the United States.[3] Another new paradigm for church was born.

If it was not for the Moravian missionaries living in community together around the fire of God's presence and intercession, willing to do anything and go anywhere for Jesus, Wesley might never have had a spiritual awakening with increased hunger to pursue God on that ship. If it was not for the Moravian missionaries who said "yes" to the call, learned to keep their eyes on Jesus and worship Him no matter the storms they faced, who knows what would have happened to the now historic church reformer John Wesley.

Though Wesley never joined the Moravians but instead started his own movement, he was still able to learn and receive impartation from them for his life and ministry.

QUESTIONS FOR REFLECTION

Impartation is like a blessing of acceleration and anointing coming from one person or group to another. Are there any people or groups God has highlighted to you to receive impartation from? What would receiving from them look like? Do you need to plan any trips to receive from them? Do you need to make time and space to read their books, watch their videos, or otherwise receive from these people who carry the anointing in a way you want to grow in?

CHAPTER 15

DIGGING THE
WELLS OF REVIVAL

S ince the Moravians have influenced and shaped my life and ministry in such a profound way, I decided to visit some of their sites to explore their legacy even further and receive impartation from being on the land.[1]

HERRNHUT (2015)

In July 2015, I traveled to Herrnhut, Germany, with a few friends from Destiny House. We stayed in the YWAM (Youth With A Mission) base there housed in an old castle. We got to visit Zinzendorf's home, which is now a museum, and explore the area. I remember being so moved by what I saw and experienced there as I imagined a community of saints doing life together around the fire of His presence. I pondered the role intercession played in this community and thought about what it would have been like to be one of the missionaries who were birthed to the nations from there. I was especially moved while visiting the prayer watchtower and also the gravesite.

ALL CELEBRATED FOR THE
GIFT OF GOD THEY ARE

There is value in stewarding stones of remembrance (see Joshua 4) and intentionally remembering the works God did before our time. At gravesites, there are literal stones of remembrance set in place. We can visit these at times to reflect upon God's faithfulness in someone's life and to encourage ourselves that if He moved in them, He can move in us in a similar way. This is a powerful act of remembering for the purpose of being inspired by the cloud of witnesses who went before us.

I was marked by what I saw and experienced during my visit to the Moravian graveyard called God's Acre. Nearly all the tombstones were the same size and shape. None out-glorified the others. Nothing but the names inscribed on the stones distinguished one gravestone from another. The only exceptions were a few larger tombstones that honored some of the elders, including the main leader, Count Zinzendorf. When I knelt to pray near his tombstone, to reflect on a life well lived, and to praise God for His faithfulness, I felt the presence and peace of God in an intense way. Honoring and remembering a saint of old nearly brought me to tears, and the presence of God overcame me.

As I reflected on Zinzendorf's life, I wondered what it would have looked like to be a part of a community that lived as a family, as a "church within a church," where everyone was celebrated for the gift of God they were, where there were no platforms, but all were on the same level before God. I didn't see any comparison within this community. Each person was important and had a role to play. No matter how seen or unseen, they were all important for the body of Christ to be able to fully function.

I wondered what that would look like today—if each person was celebrated by their community for the gift they are, regardless of position, title, job description, or role. What if a single mom doing her best to raise her kids in Christ was celebrated in the same way as one called to preach on many platforms throughout her life? What if the teacher, doctor, student, nurse, caretaker, writer, artist, cleaner, and factory worker were all celebrated equally because their identity was not in what they do but in the fact that they are a child of God? I left Herrnhut so encouraged after seeing firsthand some of the stones of remembrance that shed light on what once was there.[2]

THE CZECH REPUBLIC (2018 AND 2019)

Because the Moravian movement originated from Moravia, now the present-day Czech Republic, I wanted to dig even deeper into this movement and go to the roots of where these people originally came from. In 2018, I went to the Czech Republic for the first time with a team from Destiny House. We stayed in a castle, partnered with a 24/7 prayer and worship time hosted there, ministered, and got to visit the church where Jan Hus (1369ish–1415) regularly preached before he was martyred for defending his faith. Hus was influenced by reformer John Wycliffe (1330–1384) who was based in Oxford, England. Hus' legacy was later catalytic for reformer Martin Luther (1483-1546) and the Protestant Reformation (October 31,1517; Wittenberg, Germany).

We had such a special time together in the Czech Republic. It was like we discovered the roots of our own spiritual tribe there. The people knew how to linger in God's presence and wait on the Holy Spirit in such a tender way. We also had some beautiful moments of communion with each other on the castle grounds where the 24/7 prayer and worship was hosted. Our encounter night in the castle barn ended with us all holding hands, uniting with people from different churches. The shape of our circle morphed into a heart, which was profound because Czech Republic is known as the heart of Europe. We felt such a sweet connection with this nation and the people who birthed the Moravian movement.[3]

The very next year, I went back to the Czech Republic and did a weeklong School of Revival there to equip the saints. It was such an honor to sow back into the land I have been so blessed by.

WESLEY ROOMS IN BRISTOL (2019)

I also had a chance to visit the Wesley Rooms in Bristol, England, where John Wesley used to preach and house his circuit riders when they were passing through. He wrote many books—while standing up, I might add—from this hub created for pioneering revivalists to stay connected. The circuit riders rode horseback to stoke the flame in the existing congregations. They committed to fast two separate days each week to keep the fire burning inside. Because they were always traveling, having a safe place of refuge, where they could connect with like-minded friends and co-laborers was essential, so they wouldn't burn out. They would have meals together, talk about what the Lord had done, rest, and process theological concepts. Wesley fathered these revivalists by creating an environment where they could stay connected and be refreshed before heading back to the front lines. He cultivated a safe space for these revivalists to have family.

I was very impacted by the family structure he created there for revivalists. No doubt influenced by the Moravians' way of life, he saw a need for connection and covering. I wonder what that would look like today—to have hubs where pioneering revivalists can be themselves, live outside of the box, and ignite fires across the globe. A place where their spiritual family is lifting them up in prayer, staying connected relationally, and providing a safe space for them as they live out the unique destiny God has called them to.[4]

MORAVIAN FALLS, NORTH CAROLINA (2021)

Moravian missionaries eventually went throughout the United States and passed through a region in North Carolina that was later named Moravian Falls. I got to visit there in 2021 and spent a day on a prayer mountain, seeking the Lord in silence and nature. Aware of the Moravians' deposit years ago, many from around the world have visited Moravian Falls because they feel there is an open heaven there. Many have had encounters and revelations in this now sacred space that was cultivated by the Moravian missionaries.

QUESTIONS FOR REFLECTION

Are there any wells of revival that God is asking you to tap into or re-dig in this season? What does that look like for you? Does He want you to go and pray there? Or to read books about that well of revival? Or to write about His amazing work in that place and release the power of the testimony to others?

PART 4

MORAVIAN KEYS

I n 1727, the Holy Spirit fell in a powerful way upon the Moravians as they pursued unity. Following this encounter, the Moravians helped shape the Christian prayer movement as we know it today. The 24/7 evangelical prayer movement, the Protestant mission's movement, and even the Methodist movement can find roots or influences in the Moravians. Three hundred years later, their model for sustaining the fire of revival still holds keys for us today.

Their story is important because it shows us what it can look like to burn for Jesus and to not burn out, to keep our eyes fixed on Him no matter what storms may come our way, and to cultivate revival in family. Their legacy provides a model for how to live in unity with the body of Christ, steward the fire of God's presence, and launch people into their destinies from a place of family. Their radical commitment to the mission of Christ and to each other is an example for how to live deeply rooted in Christ and connected to His people.

There are many rich treasures we can mine from the Moravians. In this section, we will explore a few of the keys from their legacy to integrate into our own spirituality.

CHAPTER 16

ONE "YES"

The Moravian revival movement began to take form when a German nobleman chose to stop for the one. Zinzendorf's one "yes" to take in Christian David, a homeless refugee, was a decision that changed history. It opened the door for the Moravians not only to have a physical home, but to build a legacy. This one "yes" created a powerful momentum that is still impacting people hundreds of years later.

In May 2020, I was exploring the idea of doing a one-time online School of Revival intensive. I had taught the material in person at Bethel School of Supernatural Ministry, and in 2019, I did live School of Revivals in Switzerland, the Czech Republic, and Belgium. Before the world shut down in 2020, I had never considered doing a school online. This was a new idea for me, and I went back and forth with it, hesitating to dive in. I texted my friend Steve, who is a pastor in Texas, about the idea. He encouraged me to go for it and said he would commit to signing up. That was all the confirmation I needed. I said "yes" to stepping out.

When we finished our first intensive on the theme of "Family Is the Fireplace of Revival," I was done. It was a great experience. I imparted testimonies of the Azusa Street Revival, Welsh Revival, and the Moravians. Additionally, similar-hearted, present-day leaders who are also spiritual parents in my life spoke into the lives of thirty-three hungry students from around the world. When it was all over, the students told me they had found their people. When they wanted to know what was next, I wasn't sure how to respond. Their persistence caused me to reevaluate ending the school. I finally decided to say "yes" to continue the journey with them. About a month later, we did another School of Revival intensive, this time on the theme of Pioneering Revival. Then after that we did one on Azusa and then another—to the point where, a year into it, I quit my other teaching jobs to wholeheartedly dive into stewarding what the Lord had entrusted to me in the midst of a global pandemic.

When most churches around the world had shut their doors, these students were ignited with fresh fire for God and were able to stay connected to other burning ones during the isolation of lockdown. But it wasn't just about them receiving. God used this community to bring life to *me* during the lockdown as well. The Lord had divinely brought us together in a time when we all needed each other. We were able to mutually encourage each other and watch radical transformation take place. Their families' lives were even impacted because of this revival family coming together.

The following is a testimony from one person who was transformed because I was willing to give my "yes" to what I sensed the Holy Spirit wanted to do. She was also inspired to give her "yes":

> I met Jen Miskov when she came to Virginia for a weekend of ministry and events in 2019. It was an impactful and life-changing time for me and my daughter. When I saw Jen advertise an online 5-Day Ignite Azusa Challenge for School of Revival in the summer of 2020, I decided to register for it. I never would have imagined how much my life would change by that one "yes."
>
> I found a national and international family through the School of Revival. Finding my tribe opened a realm of

possibilities with God. I never would have dreamed that I would eventually become a Year 2 Pastor for School of Revival when I started! Being a part of School of Revival, and finding my spiritual family changed everything in my life. It has even had lasting impact on my husband, my five children, and my mother-in-law.

My husband saw change in my life from my pursuit after God. I became a different person, and it provoked him to jealousy. His hunger for the Lord increased. He started to fast, pray more, and seek the Lord for himself. We were now a united front, in pursuit of Jesus together for ourselves, our marriage, and our family. He watched as God opened doors for me to take big risks. He saw me say "yes" to international and national ministry trips and saw how God provided. It has caused him to take risks as well and see God open incredible doors of opportunity for him in his work and our church. We are now trusting and relying on God in every area more than before and dreaming together with the Holy Spirit!

My children started to hunger and thirst after the Lord as well. My oldest two children saw the lasting impact and changes that have taken place. They have been encouraged and challenged in their own lives. My middle daughter started to play piano and pour out her sound, her song, and her love on Jesus. She has also traveled internationally and nationally for ministry. My younger children started to sing, pray, and pursue God on their own.

My mother-in-law has also been completely transformed. Our relationship was fractured by the past, and our family didn't really have a relationship with her. During one School of Revival term, we felt the Lord ask us to open our home up for her to move in. I knew God put that on our hearts, but it was a stretch for us all. It was initially very hard on all of us. But God! He moved and healed our relationship. She has since pursued the Lord and grown so much. She even told me that she viewed me as her spiritual mother, which moved me to tears and appreciation. My 74-year-old mother-in-law learned who her Father truly was and how much He loved her. She grew with the Holy Spirit and began to pray in tongues, experience deliverance, and study the Bible. I am in awe of the transformation that has transpired! To God be all the glory!

These are just a few of the ways we have been impacted by being a part of the School of Revival family. Not only has God placed me in a tribe of fiery lovers with School of Revival, but it has spilled into *every* area of my life! We will never be the same again!

–Sara Kleppinger

That is just one example of the many testimonies that have come as a ripple effect of one "yes," and the beauty of discovering spiritual family.

REFUGEES ARE PRIME REVIVAL CARRIERS

The Moravians' legacy is tied to one rich nobleman giving his "yes" and opening space to house refugees. I didn't realize until recently how important the timing of the release of the Moravians' testimony is, as we currently have a massive refugee crisis around the globe. It makes me wonder if there's a bigger story happening around us now. I hear reports nearly daily of people fleeing their countries because of war, insurgence, danger, famine, and the list goes on. There are regular news reports of refugees who drown at sea or die of suffocation in transit or in some other accident as they attempt to get a better life. All they have is the clothes on their backs. Refugees who have fled the persecution or unrest in their own countries are prime to carry revival and be all in for Jesus. They have already lost everything; they already know how to surrender.

I wonder if our generosity and willingness to lend a helping hand to a stranger who is in desperate need might not just be an act of kindness done one to another. Perhaps there are seeds of destiny, divine intersections, and covenant communities waiting to be born. Before we turn someone away because they don't speak the same language, are poor, or are desperate for a home, it might be good to ask the Holy Spirit if He has called us to be the answer to their prayers. Some of us might not be wealthy like Zinzendorf. Some of us might even be under the weight of financial struggle ourselves, but even in that, the fact that we can read the words on this page means that we have been blessed beyond what many around the world even have access to. The next time a homeless person, a refugee, or a person in need comes across our path, and we feel the compassion of God and the prompting of the Holy Spirit to act, let's remember Zinzendorf's testimony. It was one "yes" to love the stranger in front of him that eventually catalyzed a prayer meeting that lasted one hundred years and even played a part in igniting the Great Awakening and beyond.

QUESTIONS FOR REFLECTION

Is the Lord calling you into something you have been hesitating to step into it? What would you do if you knew you couldn't get it wrong, and that God would bless you either way? What does it look like to say "yes" to the leading of the Holy Spirit today?

CHAPTER 17

STEWARDSHIP

Once the Moravian community experienced revival in family, they realized the fire needed to be kept alive so it wouldn't burn out. They saw a need to build a "fireplace" to sustain the fire. The Lord led them to steward this fire in the furnace of continual prayer and intercession in the context of covenant. When God moves in power, it's important to steward what He's pouring out.

If the Moravians had tried to steward their Pentecost fire by doing what they had always done before, that would not have cut it. They needed a new wineskin for the new wine the Holy Spirit was pouring out. Life was born and then structure was implemented to steward it, not the other way around. You can't structure to find life. Once you have life, it is then important to add wisdom to help focus it in the right direction.

Encounters welcome us into new seasons and new eras. This requires a reformation of the things we used to do before. If we have a radical encounter with God and then nothing changes in our lives, we may have missed the point or not stewarded it well for its destined purpose. The Moravians recognized that something significant had occurred in their midst when the Spirit broke out in power. They wanted the flame to increase and not to wane. Hence, a new fireplace of 24/7 prayer was birthed within community.

When you have a powerful encounter with God personally or corporately, ask Him how you are to steward that encounter. Does He want you to change a rhythm in your life? Or take something out of your schedule so you can walk in greater consecration? Is He asking you to let go of something (a commitment, relationship, rhythm)? Is He inviting you to add a new discipline to your schedule to be intentional about stewarding what He is doing in your life in the new season? If He is releasing new wine, what does the new wineskin look like?

STEWARDING PEACE IN A STORM CAN CATALYZE A GREAT AWAKENING

In the midst of a storm, the Moravians kept their eyes on Jesus and worshiped Him. When in a crisis, it is important to worship God because He never changes. In 2 Chronicles 20, King Jehoshaphat was facing the greatest army in his generation. In response, he called his people to praise God for His holiness and give thanks. While the people offered praise and thanksgiving, God was at work behind the scenes to destroy their enemies.[1]

Worship is one of the most powerful weapons of spiritual warfare. It helps us keep our focus on The One Thing, Jesus, rather than letting fear and anxiety consume us. Worship has the power to dismantle oppression and shift the atmosphere. It clears the air of evil. It creates a well of encounter for generations to step into. Most importantly, it knits our hearts together with our loving Father.

During the greatest battles of our lives, our first response should be to seek the Lord and pour out an offering of worship and praise. It is crucial to worship God in every circumstance. Fixing our affection on Jesus lifts off heavy burdens and keeps us connected to the all-powerful God who is Lord over all. Regardless of our circumstances, our resolve and consistency to worship the Almighty God should never change, because He remains the same.

You never know who might be watching how you respond in a crisis. Your decision to keep your eyes fixed on Jesus and worship Him in every storm may even catalyze the next great awakening like it did for the Moravians and their impact on John Wesley.

I remember a time nearly six years ago when I was in one of life's storms. My dad, who holds a special place in my heart, had a fall and ended up in the hospital over Thanksgiving week. We celebrated Thanksgiving at the hospital with him, but when his hospital stay ended, we had to put him in an assisted living home because he needed extra help. Instead of going back home, he went straight from the hospital to a private care home with four or five other residents. Because it was over a holiday weekend, we didn't have many options but had to get him somewhere quick.

The environment there felt so toxic. The TV was on all day, and the guy he shared a room with was super negative and even tried to attack him at one point. My dad definitely did not want to be there. He just wanted to go home, something that wasn't a viable option any longer because of the amount of care he now required. He couldn't understand this and felt imprisoned against his will in a place where strangers were now taking care of him. His mind was sharp, but his body was not able to respond the way it did before. Seeing my dad this way broke my heart. Walking into that place felt like stepping into pure heaviness and oppression. I had never had to face a storm like this before.

I remember visiting him that week. Thankfully, his roommate wasn't there at the time so we could be alone. I found a guitar and I sat there with my dad in his weakened and defeated state. He was still resisting being there and didn't understand why he couldn't come home. I strummed the guitar, and we just began to worship Jesus. As my voice cracked and I held back the tears, we sang out and glorified God together.

I will never forget the heavy *kabod* (glory) presence that began to fill the room. This was a true sacrifice of worship. I had no desire to praise the Lord. My spirit was crushed; my heart felt like it was shattered as I watched my dad in such pain. Nevertheless, we took our eyes off our-selves, off our pain, off our circumstances, and worshiped God because He is worthy of all praise no matter what storms come our way. It was one of the most powerful and weighty manifestations of God's presence I had felt in a long time, and it was during deep pain. God's presence filled that room and permeated the environment with His glory.

Not long after, we eventually got my dad into an amazing care home. He still didn't want to be there and didn't understand, but whenever I spent time with him and we sang his favorite song together, "To God Be the Glory," the manifest presence and glory of God filled the room. I was nearly brought to tears every time. There is something powerful about choosing to worship the God who never changes and always remains faithful in every circumstance, even in the most devastating of times. If we can learn, and be determined to do this regularly, we will have in our hand a key that sustains the fire within.

QUESTIONS FOR REFLECTION

What does it look like practically for you to worship Jesus during the storms in your life? How can you posture yourself to turn your eyes and affection upon Jesus in every season, good or bad? How can you build a rhythm of worship in storms and make it a core value in your life?

CHAPTER 18

MARTYRDOM

When I look at the Moravians' story, I see a people who understood Paul's words to the Philippians: "For it has been granted to you on behalf of Christ not only to believe in him, but also to suffer for him" (Philippians 1:29). They were a people willing to go anywhere and do anything for the cause of Christ, even if that meant selling themselves into slavery to reach the lost or become martyred trying. They lived Romans 12:1, which says, "Therefore, I urge you, brothers and sisters, in view of God's mercy, to offer your bodies as a living sacrifice, holy and pleasing to God—this is your true and proper worship."

German Theologian Dietrich Bonhoeffer (1906-1945) once said something to the effect of that when Christ calls us to follow Him, He bids us come and die. We are called to take up our cross and follow Him. In Matthew 16:24–25, Jesus said to His disciples, "Whoever wants to be my disciple must deny themselves and take up their cross and follow me. For whoever wants to save their life will lose it, but whoever loses their life for me will find it." The Moravians had a grasp on the true call to follow Jesus and were willing to put their lives on the line to reach people for the gospel. Many from this missional community were martyred for their faith.

ALTAR CALL

The Moravians' devotion to Jesus regardless of the cost moves me. Inspired by their example, I regularly share their testimony and invite others to a commit to a similar level of devotion. On June 24, 2022, I had the opportunity to minister at a church in Washington for a revival night, and there was one moment I will never forget.

I had prepared to share about the Moravians, but as we dove into the river of the Holy Spirit and waited upon God, He began to stir the waters in a different direction. His presence descended upon us. We were not hasty to move from that place. We remained there, fixing our eyes upon Him and leaning in to see what was on heaven's agenda for that night. While we were waiting and praying, I had a prophetic word for someone in the audience and later found out he was a pioneering leader in that region. We ministered to him and a few others.

Though I did not get to formally present my full teaching on the Moravians, I briefly shared about their story in the atmosphere of God's increasing presence. For the final ministry call, I felt compelled to do something I had never done before. I sensed that God was inviting people to demonstrate their willingness to lay down their lives for Him, even if it meant being martyred for the call of Christ, should it come to that. Technically, this is the call of every Christian when we surrender our lives to Jesus; however, there was a weightiness in the room that night that beckoned the hungry to make a renewed full surrender.

As I was exhorting them not to make this decision hastily, but to count the cost before responding, a young mother with a baby strapped to her chest *ran* from the back of the room to the altar, knelt down, and began trembling under the mighty hand of God. The fire fell upon her. Following her courageous act of devotion to Jesus, others soon rushed to the altar as well and lay face down in total surrender, willing to pay any price. Seeing the willingness in these to lay everything down for the cause of Christ marked me.[1]

If we can get to the point where we are willing to die for Christ, the way we live will look very different. I believe God is preparing the Western Church for persecution we haven't yet faced. We need to be ready. Martin Luther King Jr. once said, "If you have not discovered something you are willing to die for, then you are not fit to live." I have some dear friends who are on the front lines in other nations, and they experience some of the most horrific persecution you can imagine. They live differently. When you are on the front lines, your perspective and the way you live your life is never casual or compromising in any way. You literally are dependent upon Jesus for your very life. You have to be in tune with the Holy Spirit every second of the day and for every step you take, or it could mean your life.

I believe the Moravians' story is a prophetic call to many more burning ones around the world to lay down their lives at the altar once again. Maybe as you're reading this right now, the Spirit is stirring you to become willing to lay down your rights, comforts, plans, agendas, and even your life for the sake of the gospel. If that's you, I encourage you to lay prostrate before the Lord as a prophetic act of total surrender. Ask Him to mark you with His holy fire. Ask Him to come and fill you with His Holy Spirit. Invite Him to realign, purify, and possess every single cell in your body, so you are in perfect alignment with heaven. Repent if need be. Then yield quickly to the Holy Spirit's leading and see how God will use your laid-down life for His glory for such a time as this.

QUESTIONS FOR REFLECTION

Do you sense in your heart that you would be willing to lay down your life as a martyr for the cause of Christ if it ever came to that? How does responding to this call change the way you live today? What actions can you take this week to step into alignment with this yielded call?

CHAPTER 19

TOGETHER

The call to martyrdom did not come out of nowhere for the Moravians. It began when a people were willing to lay down their rights, die to themselves, let go of offense, and choose unity at any cost. The Moravians reconciled and became united *before* the Pentecostal fire fell. It was only after this covenantal call to unity that their movement was birthed and began to spread. The Moravians' weakness of discord later became their greatest strength in unity.

Unity is one of the most powerful weapons to defeat the enemy and see God's kingdom come. One can chase a thousand, but two working together can chase ten thousand.[1] We can host His glory in a greater measure and accomplish so much more for the kingdom together than alone.

UNITY COMMANDS A BLESSING AND INCREASES ANOINTING

Unity commands a blessing and causes anointing to increase in our lives. David highlights the importance of unity when he says:

> *How good and pleasant it is*
> *when God's people live together in unity!*

It is like precious oil poured on the head,
running down on the beard,
running down on Aaron's beard,
down on the collar of his robe.
It is as if the dew of Hermon
were falling on Mount Zion.
For there the Lord bestows his blessing,
even life forevermore.

Psalm 133

In this psalm, unity is compared to oil, and lots of it, being poured out. Oil can represent the Holy Spirit and fresh anointing. The psalmist celebrates how glorious it is when God's people live in unity.

Healing evangelist Maria Woodworth-Etter (1844–1924) experienced an increase in anointing and the manifest power of God in her ministry when she prioritized unity. During a ministry trip to Fairview, Ohio, she arrived at a church in conflict. She spent the first few days meeting in the members' homes to bring reconciliation. When the people at that church had been restored, she experienced a radical new sign in her ministry. In her own words, she said:

There had been trouble in the church for a number of years. Some of the best members had left, and the church had lost its power. I felt impressed that God was going to restore love and harmony in the church. I visited those families, and the third day of the meeting the trouble was all settled.

All who were present came to the altar and made a full consecration and prayed for a baptism of the Holy Ghost and of fire, and that night it came. Fifteen came to the altar screaming for mercy. Men and women fell and lay like dead. I had never seen anything like this. I felt it was the work of God, but did not know how to explain it, or what to say....

Those who were lying over the house as dead, after laying about two hours, all, one after another, sprang to their feet as quick as a flash, with shining faces, and shouted all over the house. I never had seen such bright conversions, nor such shouting.[2]

The atmosphere of forgiveness, reconciliation, and unity made room for increased anointing and new signs and wonders to be released in her ministry. This was the first time Woodworth-Etter experienced people being "slain in the Spirit" with trances and visions in her meetings. Unity paved the way and was a ready invitation for the Holy Spirit to be poured out in even greater measures.

UNIFIED AROUND THE BLOOD OF JESUS

As we make every effort to pursue peace with all people and prioritize the unity of the saints (Hebrews 12:14), a shift in how we see the Church might be helpful. There may be a need to reframe our understanding of Church and place it within a relational context of family. Stewarding relationships might need to become more central to our goals than building ministries or platforms. If we really believe that the kingdom of God is all about family, we will realize that we are brothers and sisters in Christ, united under the blood of Jesus. We will choose to embrace and love each other no matter how weird our "crazy uncle" or "cousin" is who worships in a completely different style than we do. In the context of family, we will ideally endeavor to work through challenges and stick together for the cause of Christ.

Jesus' last prayers before He was taken and crucified were that we as believers would be one as He and His Father are one, living in perfect unity.

> *I pray also for those who will believe in me through their message, that all of them may be one, Father, just as you are in me and I am in you. May they also be in us so that the world may believe that you have sent me. I have given them the glory that you gave me, that they may be one as we are one—I in them and you in me—so that they may be brought to complete unity. Then the world will know that you sent me and have loved them even as you have loved me.*
>
> John 17:20–23

If Jesus prayed this in His final moments before dying on the cross, it might be something for us to take seriously.

May the prayer Paul released in Romans 15:5-7 (TPT) strengthen and encourage you today:

> *Now may God, the source of great endurance and comfort, grace you with unity among yourselves, which flows from your relationship with Jesus, the Anointed One. Then, with a unanimous rush of passion, you will with one voice glorify God, the Father of our Lord Jesus Christ. You will bring God glory when you accept and welcome one another as partners, just as the Anointed One has fully accepted you and received you as his partner.*

QUESTIONS FOR REFLECTION

What does unity look like to you, and how do you cultivate it? Are there any communities you have come across that steward unity well? If so, what fruit have you seen? What does it look like in your life to pursue peace with all people and to cultivate unity in love?

CHAPTER 20

LOVE & WAR

The Moravians overcame offense and chose to honor each other despite their differences. In the face of disagreement, they chose love. Too often in the body of Christ we don't understand the real war we are in. Because of this, many times we shoot our wounded rather than lift them up. Rather than extending the hand of mercy to the hurting ones, we instead lend the hand of accusation, condemnation, punishment, and disconnection. The Church is currently being ravaged by the enemy, who is sowing seeds of offense, bitterness, and unforgiveness that are growing up into disconnection, lawsuits, slander, and a massive shift of focus off the things of God and onto the enemy's tactics.

What if instead of kicking our brother when he's down, we choose to believe for his restoration? What if instead of tearing each other down because of some offense, we choose to fight against the real enemy by standing in the gap with intercession on behalf of our brother or sister (Ezekiel 22:30)? Or what if instead of getting offended when someone hurts us because of their own brokenness, we contend for their healing?

In Ephesians 6:10–13, after writing a couple of chapters about how important it is to walk in unity and choose love, Paul encourages us to see heaven's perspective of the real war we are in.

Finally, be strong in the Lord and in his mighty power. Put on the full armor of God, so that you can take your stand against the devil's schemes. For our struggle is not against flesh and blood, but against the rulers, against the authorities, against the powers of this dark world and against the spiritual forces of evil in the heavenly realms. Therefore put on the full armor of God, so that when the day of evil comes, you may be able to stand your ground, and after you have done everything, to stand.

We must always remember what war we are truly in. Our battle is never against our brothers and sisters in Christ. *Never.* No matter how much they have betrayed us, misunderstood us, or tried to discredit us, we don't fight against flesh and blood but against principalities and powers. We have authority in Christ Jesus, through love, to tear down strongholds and move in the opposite spirit of whatever is coming up against us. When we understand that our fight is against satan and not each other, we will be able to war on each other's behalf.

What will the Church look like today if, when someone makes a decision we don't understand or agree with, we first choose love? What will happen if we become a people who give others the benefit of the doubt and believe the best about them? What will happen when we, like the Moravians, lay down our armor and the things that hold us back from each other and choose love? What will happen when we welcome the fire of God into every area of our lives? When we fight for connection as a priority above and even through disagreements and offenses?

It is important to remember that birthing anything, including revival, is always messy. In the midst of storms, God is often up to something bigger than we can imagine. We need to remind ourselves that the true war we are in is never against each other. We need each other. Life is too short to keep people out because of an offense. We need to be a people who fight *for* people, not against them. Hurting people hurt others. We need to be a people who pursue our own healing so that we can become healthy leaders. At the same time, we must learn to have compassion and mercy on those who are in the midst of God's refining fire.

FINDING THE GOLD

Healing revivalist Carrie Judd Montgomery (1858–1946) pioneered some of the earliest healing homes in the nation. In an anointed sermon she released in 1910, she captured the heart of what it means to move in the opposite spirit and choose love:

 In California we have many gold mines even yet, although they are not so plentiful as they used to be. There are two kinds of mines: one is the placer mine which contains the loose gold mingled with the sand and which therefore can easily be separated; the other is a quartz mine, where the gold is in the rock. When it is free gold it can very easily be separated from the rock, but in many of the mines there is what the miners call rebellious ore; they also call it refractory ore, and when I first heard my husband call the ore rebellious and say it was a technical term they used, I said, "That is just like some people, rebellious ore, refractory ore; the gold is there but very hard to get out." This gold is so united with baser metals that they must have a different process to get the gold free from the baser ore; they do not care anything about the baser ores, they can be burned up or volatilized, but the miners are after the gold.

Now God is after the gold in us. "I counsel thee to buy of Me gold tried in the fire, that thou mayst be rich." They have different processes now, but one process which is used a good deal is a row of furnaces through which it is put one after the other and each one is hotter than the preceding. We ask to be delivered from one of God's furnaces and we may get into a hotter one. I visited a mine and I saw the whole process. First, they broke the rock in pieces and then pulverized it, then there were large canvas sheets spread out, slightly on an incline, and the pulverized rock and ore was put on there and a stream of water was run over it, and someone stood at the top and swept it down carefully. The pulverized rock which was light went off with the water, but the metal, which was heavier, stayed on the canvas and it was swept off in little piles. It didn't look at all like gold, and you know, beloved, it is only God that can see the gold in us sometimes; I am sorry we haven't more spiritual perception to enable us to see the gold in each other. May God help us to see the gold in each other's souls!

Those sulphurets, as they call them, look something like mortar; you couldn't see any gold at all, but it was there. We went into the furnace room, and saw where they were putting it into one furnace after another; my husband is a mining man and he took me to visit this large mine that I might see all the processes.

The superintendent stood by me and we saw a lot of little sparks flying in every direction, and he explained that that was the baser metals being burned or volatilized, and then, not knowing he was uttering a great spiritual truth, he said, "When the sparks stop flying we take it out of the fire. It is finished." That was so good I looked up at my husband and said: "Why, that is the way it is with us; the Lord takes us out of the furnace when the sparks stop flying, the sparks of doubt, the sparks of fear, the sparks of impatience and of lack of love; when they stop flying then God the Great Refiner knows it is time to take us out of the furnace." Let us ask God to do His work quickly that the sparks may stop flying, but when we do see the sparks flying in ourselves or in each other shall we not be more patient now that we know what the sparks are? that they are only flying because God is working with us or working with some other soul? May God help us to be patient with each other when the sparks fly! Sparks are not always agreeable, especially when they fly upon us, but the Lord can make us patient.

Oh, I often think that if instead of getting impatient with the dear tried ones when perhaps their love fails, or their patience fails, or their faith fails, if we could only stand in love and tenderness and resist the enemy for them, claim the victory of the blood for their poor, tried souls, how much better it would be and how much faster the Lord could work with our own souls. The Lord help us! He is trying to teach us to love one another with a pure heart fervently. I understand "fervently" here, in the Greek, means to be "boiling hot" in our love. You never can have the love that keeps up to the boiling heat all the time unless you first have a pure heart. "Love one another with a pure heart fervently."[1]

We must choose to see the gold in each other and see each other how God sees us. When one part of the body of Christ hurts, we all hurt. May God give us supernatural grace for each other in times of weakness and brokenness. Just as He demonstrated mercy on our behalf, may we have grace to extend that same mercy to our struggling brothers and sisters in Christ. The world will know we are Christians by our love for each other (John 13:35).

SEARCH OUR HEARTS

Is there anyone in your community who has offended you? Anyone you need to reconcile with and forgive (Matthew 6:14–15; Ephesians 4:25–27)? Is there anyone you may have offended who you might need to approach to make things right before you dive back into worship (Matthew 5:23–24)? Is there anyone the Holy Spirit is highlighting to you right now that you need to forgive? Or that you need to reach out to and apologize to and ask for forgiveness from?

Colossians 3:12–14 says, "Therefore, as God's chosen people, holy and dearly loved, clothe yourselves with compassion, kindness, humility, gentleness and patience. Bear with each other and forgive one another if any of you has a grievance against someone. Forgive as the Lord forgave you. And over all these virtues put on love, which binds them all together in perfect unity."

Ask God to search your heart and reveal if there is any offense or unforgiveness inside you toward someone else. If He highlights someone, repent, forgive, and ask the Holy Spirit what restoring that relationship looks like (if restoration is healthy). Remember, we are called to bless our enemies and love those who have hurt us (Matthew 5:43–44; Romans 12:14–21). Are you to write them an encouraging letter, send them a gift, sow into their life or ministry? Or are you to simply repent and receive prayer from a different friend over this issue? Ask the Holy Spirit what it looks like for you to be free to love even those who have wounded you, and then respond to His leading. Reconciliation does not always mean having a close relationship with the person who hurt you, but it does mean to be at peace in our hearts and forgive, however that may look. We need the supernatural power and strength from God to love. Don't be afraid to ask Him for help.

During misunderstanding, hurt, pain, and offense, may we be a people who first run to the Lord and entrust Him with our whole hearts. May we posture ourselves with an understanding that He is in control and Lord over whatever we are facing. May we first seek to understand before being understood. May we become a people who recognize the depth of the sacrifice Jesus paid for us and, from that place of humility and gratitude, embody the love found in 1 Corinthians 13:4–8:

> *Love is patient, love is kind. It does not envy, it does not boast, it is not proud. It does not dishonor others, it is not self-seeking, it is not easily angered, it keeps no record of wrongs. Love does not delight in evil but rejoices with the truth. It always protects, always trusts, always hopes, always perseveres. Love never fails.*

And may we live what it says in 1 Peter 4:8: "Above all, love each other deeply, because love covers over a multitude of sins."

As you spend time with the Lord over the relationships He has highlighted, may the fire of God go before you and melt down any walls in your heart. May a fresh baptism of His love dismantle all offense and fear in Jesus' name. May He give you fresh courage to dive deeper into His presence and into family.

QUESTIONS FOR REFLECTION

What has God brought to the surface for you during this chapter? What actions have you taken in response to His leading? What does it look like to cultivate a new perspective of seeing people through the eyes of Christ, championing them, and fighting for them, not against them?

CHAPTER 21

DON'T EAT
YOUR FAMILY

by Heidi Baker

One Sunday morning in Mozambique, a woman who had just become a Christian several weeks before came up to share her testimony at church. The woman was very short. Her face was covered in tattoos, the beauty marks of her tribe. As far as we knew, it was the first time she had ever held a microphone. Including myself, we needed three translators to make her words understood to everyone present. She began by explaining that she had recently planned to eat her family. A dark spirit had told her that if she ate her family, her supernatural powers would grow. If she ate one of their hearts, she would gain a more powerful heart. If she ate a lung, she would gain a more powerful lung. She was not joking. She was really planning to do it. This sort of witchcraft is common in some regions, especially when food shortages and wars and bandits are raging.

In three languages, we translated that she had been planning to eat her family. Then she said, "But I came into this church, and somebody hugged me!" Soon after that she decided she was not going to eat her family after all. We translated her closing words three times: "Now I'm not going to eat my family." And she dropped the microphone.

I have spoken about her story many times because I believe the Lord wants the body of Christ to understand a simple message. We must stop eating our family. We are not to chew each other up with our words, we are not to fight with our positions, and we are not to devour one another in competition. We are not called to slander other parts of the body. We are to recognize the body for the gift it is. The lung needs the eye; the eye needs the foot. Even the least part is truly necessary (1 Corinthians 12). When we honor the whole body rightly, we begin to participate in the reality of John 17:21. Its fullness is coming!

If we as the body of Christ all over this planet would love each part of the body of Christ, not trying to force it into our own image but rejoicing wherever we recognize the Father's work, we would be one, and through this the whole world would see the Father's love.

Honoring the body of Christ around you often starts with very simple things. Ask for the Lord's guidance. He may remind you of a friend or family member with whom you should be reconciled. You may need to ask someone for forgiveness. Or you may need to go and forgive someone—not because they have earned it, but because Jesus freely forgave us (Ephesians 4:32). If anyone's wrongdoing seems hard to forgive, trust that He is more than able to strengthen you. His justice and His mercy will be enough for you.

The Lord wants to put such grace, mercy, and compassion inside of you that you would genuinely forgive every single human being who has ever hurt you or wounded you or spoken any manner of evil against you. He has more than enough love for you to forgive all others, even yourself.

LOVING OUR ENEMIES

I have friends in Mozambique who go out of their way to feed those who have stolen from them, assaulted them, and slandered them. I know saints whose hearts burn with genuine love for their persecutors. This is a true supernatural love that only God can give. This is the absolute love He wants to put inside each of us for the entire body of Christ. God wants this love to produce forgiveness wherever we have been wounded, especially by family. We are to learn how to live in peace within our natural and spiritual families, because in the end the kingdom of heaven is a family.

I was once at a large church event in a stadium. I had been praying and worshiping for several hours as the meeting went on. I felt very present with the Lord and barely noticed when someone got up on stage and began speaking about the importance of forgiveness. At first, I thought to myself, *I've already done all of that.* But as the preacher continued, suddenly I felt that the Lord was asking, "What about forgiving those who have persecuted the people in your nation?" At once I started thinking of all the terrible, unspeakable violence that various militant groups had inflicted on our neighbors. I especially remembered hearing one of our pastors tell us how his four-year-old child had been beheaded by northern rebels. Simply hearing the story had been excruciating. Struggling, I said, "Lord, I want to love them." I felt that His word in that moment was, "You only have authority where you love."

YOU ONLY HAVE AUTHORITY WHERE YOU HAVE LOVE

I feel strongly that the Holy Spirit wants to release supernatural love within each of us, so that we can love people who we may not understand how to love in the natural. In the Spirit realm, perfect love for all people is possible, because God is love. I knew I could not do this in my own strength, so I laid hands on myself and prayed with all my heart that He would let me love those who were persecuting us.

The next day, I got a call from some of our pastors in Mozambique. They had been falsely accused of terrorism by the police. On their way to a late all-night prayer meeting, they made a wrong turn. Everyone in our city had been on edge. A group of military police stopped them and began to threaten them. All of their explanations were rejected. In the end, the police beat them in the street. The pastors were attacked so severely that one of them had an eye knocked nearly out of its socket. Another's arm was broken. All of them were heavily battered.

It was a terrible tragedy. But I know our pastors and that they long for the kingdom as much as anyone I have ever met. I asked them, "Did you forgive?"

They said, "Absolutely. You know us—we forgave."

Shortly after, those military police came to our base. For the previous two years we had not been allowed to minister in the local prison because someone of a different faith was put in charge and closed the doors to us. That day the military police wrote us a letter with the names of the seven ministers who were beaten on it. Each one was granted full access again to the prison. Full access! My name was at the bottom of the list. To tell the truth, I didn't feel worthy to walk in next to these pastors. No one in my family was ever beheaded for the gospel, as some of their relatives have been. Yet the Lord, by great grace, allowed me to minister beside these amazing sons.

Because our brothers forgave persecution by those who were supposed to be protecting them, God restored all the access we had lost. The doors to the prison were reopened. We brought solar-powered audio Bibles, and any inmate who wanted to was soon able to hear the Word of God in his own local dialect. Many of those inmates had been spreading terror and violence in the region. They are invited to the kingdom too.

I've never before witnessed such love. I've never walked with anyone who taught me more about generosity and forgiveness.

BAPTISM OF LOVE

The Lord is inviting us to be baptized in love for all of His children, no matter how broken they are. We need to take bold steps into these baptismal waters. When we allow ourselves to be fully immersed, surrendering all of ourselves in the lowest place, we will rise up like eagles. The body and the blood of Christ is provision for the whole world, and we must carry it. We are no longer going to bring orphans to orphanages. We are going to bring sons and daughters home to loving families.

The Lord may send some odd-looking members of the body of Christ to you. They may live daily life very differently. The way they worship may seem different to you. Do not be afraid. Whomever God sends to you should be welcome to eat at your table. Some of them will invite you to come and eat at their tables also. Like the Jews and Gentiles of the earliest church, we must be willing to eat with one another wherever the cup and the bread of Christ unite us. As we drink the cup Christ gives us, we will experience some suffering in this world, but the joy will be far greater. He will take every trace of bitterness out of us. He Himself will wash our feet. He will cause love to possess us—love for those inside the kingdom and love for those outside.

QUESTIONS FOR REFLECTION

What stood out the most to you while reading Heidi's stories and why? What does it look like for you to position yourself to receive a radical baptism of the Father's love and to love your enemies?

PART 5

COVENANT KEYS

REVIVAL IS IGNITED, SUSTAINED, AND SPREADS IN COVENANT

After hearing from Heidi and reading about the Moravians, we can see how important it is to cultivate love and forgiveness among our brothers and sisters in Christ, and even among our enemies. We can also see how revival was ignited when the Moravians chose to set aside their differences and become unified for God's purposes. They were able to sustain the fire when they covenanted to steward it in the furnace of intercession. The fire then spread as they were sent onto the mission field from the place of prayer. Relational covenant was a key in all aspects of igniting, stewarding, and spreading the fire of revival. Covenant is like an intentional promise, commitment, or agreement made between people or God.

It is great to talk about covenant relationships and how family is the fireplace of revival, but how do we find these other burning ones? And once we find "our people," what does it practically look like to steward the fire together? What does it look like to intentionally go deeper together? In this section, we will explore ways we can partner with God to cultivate revival in family and walk in alignment with those He is gifting us to run with in this season. While there is no one set formula, there are some core covenant keys that may help to unlock greater destiny in our lives in this area.

CHAPTER 22

FINDING
YOUR PEOPLE

onnecting regularly with the wider body of Christ *and* also
meeting with a tribe within a tribe are significant keys to our
maturity. I am using the term *tribe* here to refer to a church
within a church: a smaller group of people within the body of Christ
where we can't hide but are seen, known, and celebrated for the gift
of God that we are. It is important to have people in our lives we can
mutually encourage, be vulnerable with, held accountable to, and ask
for prayer from. This heart-to-heart connection and doing life on life is
in alignment with the Word of God.[1] We usually find the people we can
go deeper with in smaller groups.

Once you have found a wider, vibrant, healthy spiritual community,
I encourage you to explore joining a small group or start your own. You
may be drawn to connect with people who are interested in learning
more about the Word or want to write songs together. Others may want
to be activated in their spiritual gifts and step out in the prophetic or
healing. Still others may simply want to cultivate a safe place to be family, gathered around God's presence where they can share a meal and
worship together. Some may want to serve the homeless or may even
want to go surfing together. The structure itself is not what is important. The regular meeting together with other sold-out Jesus lovers in a

smaller and more intimate community where you can be fully known is what will accelerate your spiritual growth.

JESUS AS OUR SOURCE

In this journey of finding our people, it is important that the foundation of a solid relationship with Jesus is laid. He must be the first one we run to in our time of need. He is our Provider and Well of Living Water. He is our best friend. No one else can satisfy quite like Him. He is faithful and will never leave us. He is the Source of all we need. David said in Psalm 62:11-12 (TPT):

> *God said to me once and for all,*
> *"All the strength and power you need flows from me!"*
> *And again I heard it clearly said,*
> *"All the love you need is found in me!"*

Wow, *all* the love we need is found in God! Though many times God chooses to meet our needs through the body of Christ, we must still run to Him first.

It is also important to recognize that as we get our satisfaction in Jesus, He has created us with a need, not just for Himself but also for each other. Even though Adam was enjoying the Garden of Eden with God and all the animals, there was still something missing. He needed Eve (Genesis 2:20-23). And God provided for his needs.

If we run to God first with our needs, everything will come into alignment. Often as we seek Him first, He will lead us by His Spirit to be vulnerable and ask for help from others in our time of need. Asking for help is healthy, takes great courage, and many times knits us closer to each other. Many times, God demonstrates His love, pours out His healing, and releases provision through the body of Christ. But if we run to each other to meet our needs without first consulting God, we remove Him from the equation and things can easily get out of order. The question we must ask ourselves is who or where are we running to for our source?

There will also be times when God allures us into the wilderness (or lonelier seasons) so that He can strip off all idols and other lovers to reinstate Himself as our Husband (Hosea 2:14-23; Song of Songs 8:5-7). Don't be surprised by these times or feel that you have done something wrong. Sometimes He leads us there simply to draw us closer to Him, to rekindle the fire our hearts, and to help us gain perspective in preparation for a new season. We must enter relationships from a place of overflow from our union with Christ, building upon the solid foundation we have in Him.

RELATIONAL ALIGNMENT

Let's explore practically how we can find and build meaningful kingdom connections with the people God wants to surround us with in this season of our lives. Note that marriage is a covenantal relationship worth fighting for. Unless there is infidelity or abuse, most of these questions are not meant to redefine that relationship but are here to help you find and build healthy spiritual family. In this journey of discovery, refinement, and relational alignment, the following questions may be helpful to process with the Holy Spirit:

- What is God saying about my relationships in this season?
- Is there anything holding me back from pursuing healthy kingdom relationships?

- Is there an invitation to pursue greater healing for my heart?

- Is there anyone I need to forgive? Be reconciled with? Or let go of?

- Are there any misalignments in my current relationships that need to be re-adjusted?

- Where am I showing up regularly to know and be known together with others? Who really knows me?

- Are these the same people I am to continue running with in this season?

- What friendships are life-giving? What friendships are draining?

- Are there any relationships that are shifting in this new season?

- Is there anyone in my life who I haven't noticed before but who might be someone to explore connecting with?

- What season am I in, and what am I running after now?

- Who do I know who is going after the same thing?

- Who do I have unusual favor with in my life?

- Who is being highlighted for me to go deeper with?

- What does it look like to build stronger connections with those highlighted?

- What does my dream community look like?

- What does it look like to be vulnerable, share my heart, and take greater risks in cultivating healthy relationships?

As you process through these questions with the Lord, make sure to spend some time waiting on Him and listening to hear His heart for your relationships in this season. If you need healing or need to forgive or be reconciled, pursue that with the Holy Spirit as a priority. I highly encourage you to do the Relationship Alignment Exercise in the Appendix to get even greater clarity for your relationships.

MOVING BEYOND DISAPPOINTMENT

If you have been hurt or rejected in the past, don't let this stop you from positioning yourself to receive healing and restorative friendships now. If you come across barriers or repeating patterns that hold you back from healthy relationships, pursue healing. Get coaching, counseling, deliverance, inner healing, prayer, or whatever is needed to get to the root of the problem and get freedom in that area.

Ask God to surround you with life-giving relationships. Be the friend you want someone else to be to you (Proverbs 18:24). Be open to God bringing people to you outside of your box or expectations. As the Spirit leads, reach out to multiple people so if some don't reciprocate, you are not discouraged, but you can connect with those who do. And if someone doesn't respond in the way you hope, this doesn't mean there will be no connection with that person ever. Sometimes it's just about timing. Remember that God is over all, and He is ultimately the One who meets all your needs.

FINDING YOUR FIT

Be encouraged in this season. You are a perfect fit somewhere—but not everywhere. You are a unique shape. There is a community out there that has a "you-shaped" hole (1 Peter 2:5). Don't get discouraged if you try to fit somewhere, and it doesn't quite feel right. Rejection is *redirection* to somewhere better. Sometimes it is also God's protection. Trust that

He is in charge and over it all. It may take a little time, and you may need to explore several communities before you find your people to run with. Be patient and endure. And once you find each other, it may take some time to build those relationships. This investment of time and heart is well worth the effort because when you find your tribe, you find your destiny. Keep going and don't give up; you might just be one risk away from finding your spiritual family to run with in this season.

It is also important to note that sometimes God might place you in a community where you remain hidden or feel you don't necessarily fit in well. Many times, pioneers or prophetic voices need to be integrated into environments they don't necessarily fit into so that something can be catalyzed in the community or in their own lives. Be faithful and obedient to God in whatever community or situation He places you in. Ask Him why He has planted you there and what His greater purposes might be for that assignment. Trust that He is your covering and knows what He is doing.

APOSTOLIC CULTURES

I have noticed in many apostolic cultures, though not all, the practical outworking of pastoral care and the emphasis on building community may seem less prominent. What I mean by apostolic culture is a revival community led by an apostolic leader who has a broader vision to see things more globally. In this type of culture, the priority and busyness of pioneering revival can easily overshadow the importance of building healthy spiritual family. This does not mean it's not happening within the leadership behind the scenes, just that it might manifest itself differently than what you need.

If you feel drawn to run with a certain community and the value for building spiritual family is not being lived out or emphasized in the way you hope, don't be afraid to start something yourself that will meet your needs. God may want you to create a small group of burning ones so that you can live true to your core values and provide a space for others to also find family. Remember, we are all part of the same body of Christ and each of us has a unique gift we bring. Don't be afraid of different. At the same time, don't compromise or shrink back from being the gift you are called to be. Make sure you are in a healthy environment where you are encouraged to soar and can thrive.

ALIGNING HEARTS

In this hour, I believe it is crucial that we find healthy spiritual community and get planted where God leads. Then, we need to be vulnerable and wholeheartedly run together after the things of the Spirit. I've noticed that many times as I pursue Jesus with everything inside of me, when I look to my left and my right, I find others running on the same path right beside me. These have become some of my most precious friends. I wasn't necessarily looking for them when this happened, but God provided them along my journey of seeking Him first (Matthew 6:33).

There is a massive tsunami wave of revival increasingly upon us. God is aligning people with their tribe so they can mature in Christ. He is knitting hearts together so they can help steward the surge of new believers and welcome them into the family. You are an important part of what God is releasing over our generation in this unique *kairos* moment.

On this journey toward deeper connection, may you have the grace to embark with fresh expectancy. May He heal any wounds, uproot any disappointments, and resurrect hope within you. I release blessing, favor, discernment, and divine appointments in finding the kindred spirits you were born to run with for such a time as this. I declare acceleration over you as you seek Jesus first and grow deeper with the community God highlights to you in this season. I pray that God would place you in a healthy spiritual family and in covenant relationships where you are known, loved, and championed to run your race for His glory.

QUESTIONS FOR REFLECTION

Are there any disappointments you need to release to God? Any hope deferred He wants to heal? What does it look like for you to dream, believe again, and pray for God-given friendships and divine alignments in your relationships? What did God show you when going through the questions to discern relational alignment in this chapter? Who are some of the people He highlighted for you to be more intentional with? What can you do today to take the first step toward these deeper kingdom connections?

I want to remind you to prioritize going through the Relationship Alignment Exercise in the Appendix if you haven't already. I truly believe and pray that God will use this to help bring breakthrough and alignment for the kingdom relationships He has awaiting you.

CHAPTER 23

CULTIVATING REVIVAL IN FAMILY

Once God begins to connect you with your spiritual family in this season, explore together what it might look like to cultivate the fire for His presence together. Most revivals began when a small group of burning ones gathered to encounter more of God. There are several core values and rhythms I have learned in my years of ministry and in studying revivals that have helped contribute to cultivating revival in family.

RHYTHMS

When I was leading Destiny House from 2012–2019, we all lived together, worshiped together, and ministered together. You can read more about Destiny House in my book *Walking on Water* or on my website.[1] While living together can be very messy at times, it is also one of the most beautiful experiences a person can have. Throughout this time of doing life on life, I learned that being a part of a spiritual family accelerates growth and that we can't step into the fullness of our destinies apart from our people.

Our Destiny House community—which at one point had twenty-one people living in intentional community together (which is way too many, by the way)—embraced several patterns of life together. Stemming from our core values of glory, honor, destiny, and consecration, the following three rhythms, or ways of life modeled after Jesus, were implemented in Destiny House in the past decade.[2] We fasted together on Mondays to cultivate hunger for God. Then that same evening, we broke the fast with a family meal and a time to connect with each other. We also had an open Friday morning worship and ministry time, where anyone was welcome to join. There, we gathered around God's presence and ministered together as a family. Most of those who lived in the house were ministry school students, so this level of commitment worked well for us.

Those in the book of Acts who met together *daily* (Acts 2:46–47; 5:42), the Moravians, and even our group at Destiny House embraced certain rhythms to help cultivate revival in family. There may be some keys from these rhythms that can be adapted and integrated into your community to help foster a revival culture. Though physically living together may not always be accessible or ideal, it is still possible to cultivate revival in family, as we have experienced in our School of Revival online family as well as with those who did not live at Destiny House.

In cultivating revival in family, it's important to realize that it's not about being bound to a structure. It's about welcoming the Holy Spirit to lead you and your community into greater depths of His presence and glory, however that looks. It's about establishing and embracing the core values God forms in you and then expressing those in your own unique context. I hope and pray that the patterns we have embraced will inspire you to intentionally and creatively gather with your people to pursue Jesus in a special way. Here is the practical outworking of our core values.

1. Cultivate Family (Connection)

As an intentional revival community at Destiny House, we would regularly set aside one night a week exclusively for family time. This included making and sharing a meal together, spending time catching up and sharing testimonies, connecting, and praying for one another if needed. What happened during our family nights looked different each week. The primary goal was not ministry, but connection. Impartation, teaching, and equipping sometimes happened, but they were not the regular focus of these times, since most in our community were getting these things every day at their ministry school. Some of our family nights turned into the Holy Spirit falling upon us in a special way and ended in pure worship to Him. Other times, they ended with us in a big circle and each person making up a spontaneous rap song. Another time, we all went out for ice cream.

One key to consider integrating into your community is creating a safe place with regular time set aside simply to be with each other, share a meal, connect at a heart level, have fun, and be family. Vulnerability and creativity are also important aspects you can build into your rhythms for connection. When people feel safe and are seen, known, and loved, they will be healed and become who they are destined to be.

Ask God what it looks like to build a culture of healthy spiritual family around you.

2. Cultivate Hunger (Fasting & Feasting)

Another element we integrated into our community was regularly fasting and feasting. Jesus did both. Because we wanted to grow in our hunger for more of God, on Mondays we would skip breakfast and lunch to fast. Then in the evening, we would break our fast with dinner together. This worked well as a potluck. Everyone got involved and contributed to the communal meal. In our School of Revival family, we continue this

143

rhythm of fasting together on Mondays. Then whenever we get together for in-person retreats or ministry trips, we feast around the table.

Many revivalists experienced their defining moments while on a fast. Many revivals have also been birthed when a small group of people went on a corporate fast together, as seen with the Azusa Street Revival. There have also been other times when people have encountered the Holy Spirit crashing in with power while feasting together with their spiritual family. This happened to John Wesley and his friends one New Year's Eve at the love feast prayer meeting that birthed the Great Awakening. He and all his circuit riders later adopted a rhythm of fasting two days each week to keep the fire burning. A blend of fasting and feasting is powerful when done together in community.

3. Cultivate Space for Encounter (Worship) & Minister Together

Our community also regularly set aside a time each week to open our doors to host a worship encounter time together as family. This was open to all ages, and we especially loved it when children could join in. Dance and creativity also had a special place in the worship gathering.

These gatherings weren't necessarily about seeking answers to prayer or praying for healing. They were times set apart primarily to minister to Jesus (Psalm 27). Even the song choices were all about loving Him. While praise, thanksgiving, and crying out to God are all good, our emphasis was mostly on *adoration.* We wanted to set down our agendas, our problems, and simply worship Him because He is worthy no matter what we are going through. We also encouraged all present to turn off their phones or put them on airplane mode, so that we could go on a journey together without any distractions.

At the start of our times together, we briefly welcomed guests and had a few people share testimonies. Someone from the house would then give a brief word from the Bible (5–10 minutes), and then we went straight into worship, sometimes for hours. Influenced by the Welsh Revival, our meetings were worship focused and given over to the leading of the Holy Spirit. We positioned ourselves to encounter God. As we dove into the river of the Holy Spirit and yielded, our meetings looked different every week. Sometimes everyone would shout praises, and other times we would all be on our faces in the *kabod* glory, where no one could even talk because His presence was so weighty.

Ministering to Jesus and flowing in the Holy Spirit together as family each Friday forced us to pursue unity with each other before hosting the worship encounter, so that we could steward the glory of God unhindered. It was powerful to do this week after week in the context of spiritual family. Part of this practice was learning to show up in community no matter what was going on in our lives. We learned to consistently love Jesus in the context of family. Stewarding this well of encounter also sharpened us to stay unified and learn how to better flow with the Holy Spirit.

In that atmosphere of freedom in the Holy Spirit, we learned His ways and how He moved. It felt like we were in the school of the Spirit. It became a greenhouse for us where we could step out and explore our spiritual gifts. Taking risks, getting it wrong, learning, growing, and making space for the Holy Spirit to move in a safe environment where risk was celebrated, all accelerated our spiritual growth. Creativity was stirred as we made space to worship God with all our hearts, minds, souls, spirits, and bodies. Prophetic art, painting, and dance were also a regular part of our worship.

Many times, as we poured out our love to Jesus, the Holy Spirit would come in a powerful way and mark us with the Father's transforming love and fire. It was normal for people to weep as He healed deep things in their hearts without anyone even praying for them. Physical and emotional healing regularly occurred, as did other unique signs and wonders like money appearing in someone's pocket, gold dust, revelations from heaven, voices being restored, hearts unlocked, prophetic acts, and revival in people's hearts. We never sought after the signs—we sought Jesus—and these things came as a result.

FRUIT

Cultivating an atmosphere of family, hunger, and encounter within Destiny House proved to be catalytic in our lives and ministries. Many were changed, healed, delivered, and catalyzed into their destinies, all from these precious times of worshiping together and doing life together as family.[3]

In the context of worshiping God with spiritual family each week for over seven years, I learned how to better flow with the Holy Spirit. That time was one of the best ministry trainings I have ever received. One of the primary things I learned from living in intentional community around the presence of God is that the keys of our destiny are found in intimacy with God and in interconnectedness with the body of Christ. I have since taken and integrated the core values I learned in Destiny House into the foundations of my new ministry communities, especially School of Revival.

Taking on a different structure, the core values developed at Destiny House have been adopted in the School of Revival family under the names of family, fire, and revival.[4] Though they are called something else, the heart behind these has remained the same. In School of Revival, we make space for people to connect as family to pray and prophesy over each other in Zoom breakout rooms and during our in-person retreats. We have corporate times of debriefing after revival sessions, where we lean into God's presence and wait upon the Holy Spirit together. We have activations where people are challenged to step out in faith to synergize what they have learned. We fast together on Mondays and have regular prayer meetings. We have creative expressions, where people vulnerably share their hearts through various forms of creativity in a safe, loving, and encouraging environment. We also do regular ministry trips together.[5]

Though School of Revival began primarily as an online community, cultivating revival in family has still had a radical impact, despite a different context. Below is a testimony of how staying true to our core values of family, fire, and revival has produced some amazing fruit:

> Being a part of the School of Revival family has had a significant impact on my spiritual walk. I was a mature Christian pastor but was seeking a group of people who were hungry for the fire, power, and intimacy of fellowship with God. I bought a book by Jen Miskov called *Fasting for Fire* while at a conference. I read the book and learned about School of Revival. After I emailed Jen, I was invited to join a School of Revival online intensive called Harvest.
>
> I quickly learned that the culture of School of Revival was to give your total "yes" and pursue God with reckless abandon. Everyone is encouraged, championed, and inspired to walk out the teachings through our interactions and activations. There is regular prayer and prophecy over each other. The entire experience is like joining a family of people who are sold out, surrendered, and pursuing an intimate love of God and others. We champion each other, cheer each other on, pray for each other, and ignite passion for Jesus and revival!
>
> By being a part of this spiritual family, I have been challenged to evangelize, pray in tongues more, and I even started a ministry among the homeless in my city. This

came to pass after I had an encounter with the Holy Spirit at our School of Revival in-person retreat at the Home of Peace in Oakland, California, in 2022. I was consumed with His peace, anointing, and Spirit and prophesied over. As a result, I felt called to sell everything and live a life of consecration and ministry. I was already transitioning our small church because I felt called to do evangelism but was unsure what that would look like. God began to birth a desire within me to reach out to the homeless with His love and forgiveness. I was unsure how to go about reaching them and began to fast and pray. Our School of Revival family fasts every Monday, and they were praying for me as well.

Then, one Sunday I stepped out to feed the homeless and preach the gospel. From that one "yes," every Sunday we get together under a freeway bridge where I share the gospel and feed the homeless. We have up to 150 each week who come out. Other churches have also partnered to help. This was all a direct result of joining the School of Revival family, where we are all encouraged to do the ministry of Jesus while staying intimately connected to God and others in our spiritual family.

–Pastor Jeff LaPorte

That is just one testimony of what can happen when creating an atmosphere of revival in family. As people grow closer to God and to each other, they are naturally launched into their destinies. Pastor Jeff's testimony is a perfect example of the importance of extending the invitation to come and sit at the table—welcoming people to be seen, known, and belong; preparing a feast for them; and then releasing them to feed others from their overflow.

QUESTIONS FOR REFLECTION

Which of the core values or rhythms mentioned in this chapter resonate with you the most and why? What other core values that were not mentioned above do you want to build upon? Who else do you know who shares these same values? How can you begin to cultivate and integrate these core values into your life and ministry—and invite those with a similar passion to join you?

Consider adding the rhythm of fasting on Mondays alongside our School of Revival family.

You also may want to explore hosting or planning a time with a few other burning ones to share a meal and then worship and adore Jesus together. Have no other agenda than to welcome the Holy Spirit, worship Jesus, and wait upon God together. Then, see how He wants to move.

I also encourage you to do the Core Values Activation in the Appendix to get greater clarity in defining the core values that are important to you.

CHAPTER 24

KEYS FOR SUSTAINING PERSONAL REVIVAL

C ultivating revival in family, stewarding a heart of worship in all circumstances, and praying in tongues regularly can profoundly shape our spirituality, keep us focused on the face of Jesus, and help increase the flame within. Here are a few more keys I've learned in how to sustain and steward personal revival.

1. STAY FULL OF THE OIL OF INTIMACY

In Matthew 25:1–12, we see the story of the wise and foolish virgins. This parable is symbolic of making sure we steward the oil of intimacy in our lives and keep the fire burning. If we try to rely upon the overflow of another's walk with Christ, it won't get us to where we need to go. We must personally make sure to invest time in our secret place with Jesus, getting filled up by Him with the Holy Spirit and fire. There is no shortcut to building intimacy with Jesus; it requires time and an open and vulnerable heart. In John 15:1–8, we see that all fruitfulness flows from intimacy with Christ. We must readily stay connected to our Source.

2. KNOW THE BIBLE

We must be a people who know the truth deeply, especially in the midst of the increasing delusions, lies, and deceptions of the enemy. People who work at banks know when there is a counterfeit bill because they handle so much real money. When we are saturated in the truth, we will know when something is off. The shaking in our world will only increase. Our feelings and emotions may vary. We need to stand strong on the Word of God, which is a solid rock. We must read it, eat it, breathe it, meditate on it, memorize it, and make declarations with it. Audio versions of the Bible are also a good way to get the Word hidden in our hearts.

3. STEWARD ENCOUNTERS AND GOD'S VOICE

We need to learn to discern and steward the voice of God through His Word, encounters, and the prophetic voices speaking into our lives. When God touches you, linger in that space. Don't shift or transition too quickly out of an encounter with Him. Don't jump right into a conversation with someone, look on social media, or get distracted another way. Allow what He has just deposited within you to permeate to the deepest levels. Meditate on what is good, and it will have a greater effect on you. Journal what He shows you. When God speaks to you, obey Him immediately and keep your heart tender toward Him. Steward prophetic words over your life. If possible, try to audio record them, and then listen to them, writing them out and praying over them until they become a reality.

4. FAST

Develop a rhythm of weekly or regularly fasting to keep the fire burning. You would be surprised at the radical shift that regular fasting can have in your life. Jesus regularly fasted, and we are called to walk in His footsteps. Many revivals, encounters, or defining moments in revivalists' lives came while the person was on a fast. See my book *Fasting for Fire* for more on this topic. This book has testimonies as well as many practical tools to help get you started. It reintroduces fasting as a lost art of feasting upon God and an invitation to greater intimacy with Jesus.

5. LEARN TO WAIT ON THE HOLY SPIRIT

Psalm 46:10 says, "Be still, and know that I am God." How many times do we stop talking, moving, planning—to simply be with God and sit in His presence?[1] Too many of us think we have to strive, contend, or push to see God move. But what if, rather than trying to make things happen on our own, we just spend time with the Holy Spirit, listen to what is on God's heart, are fully yielded, and respond to how He is leading us? What if, like Moses, we choose not to go anywhere, not even into revival or into our destinies, if He doesn't go with us (Exodus 33)? What if we become a people who are led by fire in the night and cloud in the day, a people who won't move anywhere without His presence (Numbers 9)? Or those who flow in the river of His Spirit and easily follow where He is leading (Ezekiel 47)?

6. EMBRACE RHYTHMS OF REST, RUN, RELEASE

It is important to discern what season you are in so you can steward it well in preparation for the upcoming season. Many times in life, there are seasons when you rest, run hard, and then release or birth new things. This is cyclical in nature. It is important to recognize your season and make any necessary adjustments so you can be sure to get what you need during that time. The Sabbath is not only biblical, but it is also a key for unlocking greater creativity in our lives. Embracing the Sabbath, having fun, eating healthy foods, exercising regularly, and stewarding our bodies which are temples of the Holy Ghost (1 Corinthians 6:19), are essential to running hard and finishing well.

7. SURROUND YOURSELF WITH OTHER BURNING ONES

Most of this book has highlighted this key. A single flame alone might burn for a little while, but for that flame to increase and not die out, it needs to unite with other flames. The more flames that come together, the greater the fire and likelihood that your flame will not wither. I've seen too many people be a part of a great culture, environment, or ministry school for a season, get radically impacted, and then return to their homelands without intentionally finding and running with other sold-out burning ones. Soon their fires begin to wane or even worse, they go back to the lifestyles they had before God encountered them powerfully. We need to find other passionate Jesus lovers wherever God places us. The great thing now is that even if you can't find any in your hometown, you can run with other burning ones in online communities. Even at a distance, they can provide support for you to help you keep your fire burning. Ask God to surround you with spiritual mothers and fathers, kindred-spirited burning friends, and others you can encourage.

8. STEWARD THE POWER OF THE TESTIMONY

Another way to build up your faith and keep the fire burning is to recount and thank God for the testimonies of His faithfulness in your life and how He's come through in the past. Do this in whatever way works best for you. You could hang a picture that reminds you of a breakthrough or of His radical provision, write down testimonies on 3x5 cards so you can encourage yourself, or listen to a recording of a song, a significant moment, or a prophetic word that touched you. Steward these stones of remembrances (Joshua 4). By remembering testimonies of God's faithfulness in the Bible, in revival history, in your own personal history with Him, or in others' lives, you are prophesying into future breakthroughs and radical acts of faith.

9. LEARN HOW TO DEAL WITH DISAPPOINTMENT

One of the biggest things I've noticed that takes Christians out or sidelines them is when they fail to deal with disappointment well. Some might suffer loss, have something happen to them they don't understand, or step out in faith for something that doesn't happen. Rather than grow and learn from that experience, and trust that God will turn it around for their good, many get discouraged, disillusioned, build up distrust against God, or condemn themselves as failures. If we really believe all the promises found in Romans 8 and have a healthy perspective of God the Father, we won't turn to bitterness or embrace disappointment. Instead, we will deepen our connection with the Father and learn to trust Him even more. I encourage you to memorize portions of Romans 8 and meditate on the truths found there so that you will not be shaken.

10. CHOOSE UNITY AND LOVE

This is important both on a personal and corporate level. Strive to be at peace with all people and take the road of humility again and again (Romans 12:18; Philippians 2). Trust God to vindicate you when you've been wronged. And just as Christ forgave you, also forgive others.

11. DON'T BE AFRAID TO SHINE

Finally, don't be afraid to shine (Isaiah 60). God has appointed some to be leaders in our generation. Not everyone is given the same amount of influence, favor, resources, or anointing for leadership. Not everyone was called to lead the Israelites out of Egypt—but Moses was. Then God appointed Joshua to lead them even further into their Promised Land. Be the gift God has called you to be, however that might look. Do the assignments He has entrusted to you without making excuses, making yourself look smaller, or sabotaging His call on your life (Ephesians 2:10).

QUESTIONS FOR REFLECTION

In addition to what we talked about in this chapter, what other keys can help you steward the fire in your heart? Which keys are you doing well in? Which do you need to develop further? Is there someone in your life you can invite into this journey to help keep you accountable in the areas you want to grow in?

CHAPTER 25

HESED

In the book of Ruth, we see a powerful covenant bond that later played a pivotal role in Ruth's ability to step into her destiny. When Naomi tried to send her two daughters-in-law back to their homes following the death of her sons, they both wept and didn't want to leave her. When she urged them a second time, Orpah said goodbye and returned to her people and gods, but Ruth clung to Naomi and said:

> *Don't urge me to leave you or to turn back from you. Where you go I will go, and where you stay I will stay. Your people will be my people and your God my God. Where you die I will die, and there I will be buried. May the Lord deal with me, be it ever so severely, if even death separates you and me.*
>
> Ruth 1:16–17

When Naomi saw that Ruth was determined to stay by her side, she stopped trying to get her to leave. Long story short, Naomi advised Ruth to lie at the feet of a wealthy kinsman, Boaz, who in turn pursued and married her. This placed Ruth in the family line of King David, who would be her great-grandson, and it also put her in the family lineage of Jesus Himself (Matthew 1:1–7). On the other hand, after Orpah returned home, she married and bore children. It is believed that Goliath came from her family lineage.

The word *hesed* in Hebrew is used in Ruth 1:8, 2:20, and 3:10 and is translated as "lovingkindness," "mercy," "love," and "compassion." The first two uses are in reference to God's lovingkindness. Then in 3:10, Boaz uses this word to describe Ruth's kindness. *Hesed* is used around 250 times in the Old Testament, half of those being in the Psalms, and is usually the theme of God's lovingkindness, loyalty, and faithfulness. Brian Simmons, translator of *The Passion Translation*, describes it like this:

> *Hesed* is God's overflow of mercy, kindness, and love. It is limitless and extravagant. There is nothing you can do but receive it. It comes with no strings attached for those who are undeserving. I really believe that the inexpressible Hebrew word *hesed* is the greatest word in the Bible. It is an ocean of meaning in a drop of language. It is a word beyond words. It is a love past finding out. It is love, kindness, faithfulness, tenderness, compassion, and mercy times infinity![1]

Hesed is also a concept that embodies what a true covenant and loving bond can look like between people. The relationship between Ruth and Naomi illustrates this theme so well. Jonathan also demonstrated this covenantal love with his friend David, even though God's favor upon David meant Jonathan wouldn't inherit the throne. There is something special that happens when the people God has brought together decide to make a covenant, or promise, to stand with each other no matter the cost. Many aligned in covenant relationships tend to be launched into their destinies in remarkable ways.

YOUR DESTINY IS HIDDEN IN YOUR PEOPLE

Our destinies are found in Jesus first and foremost. After that, they are also catalyzed within each other. We can't accomplish the fullness of our God-given destinies alone. The Moravians could not have stepped into the fullness of their destiny without Zinzendorf. And he could not have fulfilled his without them. Zinzendorf's God-given assignment and purpose were intertwined with the Moravian refugees. When we find our covenant people and establish meaningful connections, our destinies naturally unfold.

There is always an exchange of gifts that takes place when we unite with our brothers and sisters in Christ (1 Corinthians 14:26). If you are drawn to a certain person or they are highlighted to you, it may be because they hold a key to your destiny. Other times, it may mean you hold a key to theirs. Pay attention to the people you are drawn to and ask the Holy Spirit to bring greater revelation to why He is pointing them out to you. It could be that gold is waiting to be discovered in that relationship.

There are people God has placed in your life in this season that you need to fulfill your destiny. And there are people who need you. If you are not currently intertwined with your tribe, you are a missing piece of the tapestry God is designing and weaving together in the body of Christ. The prayer released in Ephesians 3:20 for God to do exceedingly abundantly above all we could ask, hope, dream, or imagine is a promise given to a people, not a person. It says He will do abundantly above all *we* could imagine, not all *I* (one person) could imagine. Though He loves to bless us individually, there is a different sort of synergy and exponential expansion when the blessing falls upon a community unified together for His purposes. God has ordained for you to be alive for such a time as this and to be perfectly positioned where you are for a reason. It is not an accident you are where you are today, surrounded by the people God has placed in your life.

QUESTIONS FOR REFLECTION

Ask God to reveal His strategic, divine purpose over you at this time. Why has He planted you in the region you currently live in? Is there a greater purpose than you can see for why He placed you there? What might He be orchestrating for you behind the scenes? Why has He connected you with the people in your life? Is there anyone He is highlighting for you to go deeper with? How do you define covenant?

CHAPTER 26

MIRACLE HOUSE

The following is a personal testimony of what God has released in my life through a covenant relationship in this *kairos* moment. Heidi Baker has been a spiritual mother in my life for over two decades now.[1] Being in a devoted relationship with her has resulted in many breakthroughs in my life and ministry. I pray you are blessed and that your faith is stirred as you read this recent account of God birthing the miraculous in covenant.

REFLECTING ON TESTIMONIES OF GOD'S FAITHFULNESS

In early 2022, I was reflecting on the anniversaries of some profound things God did in my life a decade earlier. In 2011, I graduated from Birmingham University in England with my PhD and then moved back to Southern California. Toward the end of that year, I moved by faith to Redding, California, and there, following a long fast, I was ordained by Heidi Baker on New Year's Eve. One week later, I began a project on the Apostolic Inheritance of California, where I interviewed Heidi as well as Bill Johnson. In early February 2012, I launched my first Writing in the Glory workshop at a local coffee shop with three other people. During this unique birthing season, I had no car, little money, and was sleeping on a blow-up mattress on my friend's floor, contending and believing for breakthrough while being stretched beyond anything I had experienced before.

During this season in February, I also stepped out in radical faith to found what later became known as Destiny House. In March of that same year, I released my fourth book *Life on Wings: The Forgotten Life and Theology of Carrie Judd Montgomery (1858–1946),* and later in the year, I began working on the book *Defining Moments* with Bill Johnson.

During one of the most vulnerable and stretching times of my entire life, when I was living off my credit card, God birthed many things that are still bearing fruit to this day. Be encouraged if you're currently being stretched right now; it is probably because you are pregnant with a promise, and God is about to birth something amazing in and through your life. In the stretching, He is refining and preparing you to carry what He wants to birth.

Fast-forward ten years later to early 2022. Because of the weight of these ten-year anniversaries (Writing in the Glory, Destiny House, the filming for Apostolic Inheritance of California project, along with several book projects) I felt led to reconnect with Heidi and invite her to pray into the next decade with me. I met up with her and her longtime friend on Saturday, February 5, 2022. As we sat on the beach, Heidi shared testimonies of house breakthroughs in her life. She prophesied over us and prayed that God would also bring us breakthrough in that area. Then she told me, "God wants to give you a house, but you have to start looking."

I had tried to buy a house by faith in Redding years ago and explored owning a home more recently, but nothing ever came to pass. What she said to me in that moment was not on my immediate radar or anything I was considering at the time. I had forgotten about my dream to get a home because it felt so impossible and out of reach. I honestly didn't do much with her prophetic word because I didn't have the resources, and

Heidi and I at the beach the day she prophesied over me about the house.

I was comfortable where I was. However, when I found out Heidi was coming back to town in June to speak at my church, I realized I better get the ball rolling before she got there. God has regularly used Heidi to speak into my life during significant transitions, and I wasn't about to miss what He might want to do.

It took me over three months to finally take the first step forward in response to her prophetic word and apply for a home loan. God connected me with an incredible loan officer who prayed for me throughout the whole process and was such a gift to me in this journey. I got approved for a loan in mid-June, which was a miracle in and of itself. As I was searching online for homes, I realized if I was going to step out in faith for a home, I needed to love it and it needed to feel like a refuge and retreat. I couldn't come near affording anything in Orange County, so I ended up looking for homes in the nearby mountain area where I would regularly go to unplug and write in tiny houses in nature.

"I DON'T REALLY NEED TO BUY A HOUSE AND I DON'T HAVE THE MONEY"

I had booked a Getaway tiny-house stay in the mountains about an hour from my family's house and decided to look at homes in the nearby area since I was already out there. My real estate agent drove all the way up to the mountain to show me some homes, but nothing really caught my eye. I remember telling him, "I don't really need to buy a house. I am not in a hurry, and I don't have the money. The only reason I am looking is because my spiritual mother told me that God wants to give me a house, and I need to start looking to position myself for the miracle."

After every house fell short of my expectations, I began to feel bad that my agent had come all that way for nothing. At the end of a discouraging afternoon, I asked him to come see where I was staying, so he

One of the Getaway mini-houses I used to stay in to write and pray.

could get a better idea of what I was looking for. I showed him the inside of the tiny house. It had one big window looking out into nature. I told him I wanted something like that. He probably thought I was crazy, but I knew the only way this was ever going to happen was if a miracle came straight from heaven. And I wasn't going to settle for anything less than knowing it was a miracle.

As the weeks went on, I was busy traveling, and honestly, I was a bit discouraged after our first failed attempt to find the right house. I didn't look for houses as vigilantly as before and only looked online here and there. Late July, as I was getting ready to go up to Redding for the first time since the lockdown, my agent reached out to see if I had any time to look at homes again. I literally had only Saturday, July 30, open before heading out of town again. I had been watching one home that I thought I really liked and saw that the price kept dropping. I wondered if this could be "the one." He encouraged me to look up some other homes nearby too, since we were already making the trip out there.

We met up and looked at a few homes, but I didn't connect with any of them. Then we went to see one house that was way over my budget but had four massive windows looking straight into the forest. I really liked the home; however, it was $200,000 over the price range I wanted to spend, and I still hadn't seen the original house I had my heart set on.

When we finally made it to the house I had been watching online the one that was more in my "faith" price range, it was nothing like I thought it would be. I didn't like the location or anything about the house. It was a clear "no." We still had another couple of homes to check out after that one. As we looked at a few other options, my heart kept leading me back to the earlier home with the four big windows looking into nature.

At the end of our house-hunting day, it was obvious to me that I really loved the house that was outside of my "miracle budget." Though the price was higher than I was thinking I could do, the loan I was approved for would just cover it. Because I had a prophetic word from my spiritual mother that God was giving me a home, I believed that we were in a *kairos* moment, and I felt I had found my treasure hidden in a field, I decided to trust in God and take the next step of faith.

A couple of days later, on Monday, August 1, I put in an offer to buy the home. The seller didn't come down on the price much at all, but he did agree to sell me the home, so I could avoid any potential bidding wars. The next day, while I was at my songwriting home group led by my friends Michael and Ivey Ketterer, I signed the contract to purchase the home. My home group had been praying for me every step of the way. I needed their faith, encouragement, and prayers in this process.

There was no way I could close escrow at the end of the month and make the final payments of closing costs without the miraculous intervention of God. I was trusting that He would make a way where there was no way. I was taking each step as far as I could. Praise God, just in the nick of time, He provided through the body of Christ in a special way. By the due date, I was able to pay all the closing costs and officially close the loan to buy the house.

TRIPLETS

On August 30, during the same week my house was closing, I had a mini-release party for my tenth book, *All Who Are Thirsty*, with my home group. They celebrated with me and even wrote a song about the book, which was so special. The very next day, I signed a stack of documents to finalize the loan, and on September 1, I launched our School of Revival intensive on the Apostolic Inheritance of California. The video interviews I did ten years earlier with Heidi Baker and Bill Johnson were finally going to be released. My plan was to teach this School of Revival online intensive from my own California home, carrying the authority

of ownership and putting a stake in the ground in the soil of California. Of course, there were some delays and complications near closing, which pushed the move-in date back.

The very next day, September 2, I drove by faith toward the house, praying that by the time I got there, the county would have recorded the sale so I could legally move in. While on the drive there in the afternoon, I got the call from my agent telling me that everything went through, and the home was officially mine! I had the internet set up that night and then taught the final sessions of our first School of Revival intensive of the new school year from my own California home the following day!

This all happened on Labor Day weekend which was so fitting. I felt like I had just birthed triplets: my tenth book *All Who Are Thirsty* (that had been sitting on my computer for nearly ten years), the Apostolic Inheritance of California training I had been waiting ten years to release, and my Miracle House—all in the same week.

Oh, and by the way, one more thing I forgot to mention. When Heidi was prophesying over me earlier in the year, she told me that her first home was in the exact same mountain town I had already been going to regularly to write in the tiny houses, and it was the same town where I also got my first home. Now if that's not some crazy Holy Spirit synergy, I don't know what is!

All that to say, there is something powerful in honoring those you are in covenant with. Ruth submitted to Naomi and thus stepped into the lineage of Jesus and gained an inheritance. I took Heidi's advice seriously in a *kairos* moment, and God opened every door. I am so grateful Heidi shared her testimony and prophesied over me that day in February on the beach. I am grateful for all the "midwives" who partnered in prayer and for those who sowed into making this dream become a reality. The Miracle House would not exist without the body of Christ coming together in faith for this miracle.

COME UP HIGHER

I am now finishing up this manuscript in my Miracle House, looking out four massive windows into nature and enjoying perfect silence. This home is beyond anything I could ask, hope, dream, or imagine. My new home doesn't have just one window peering directly into nature, but four. This can be symbolic of Revelation 4:1 and the invitation to come up higher into heavenly realms. I don't know about you, but this just demonstrates the goodness of our God to do exceedingly abundantly above and beyond our deepest desires simply because He loves us. The home feels like it was handcrafted just for me, hidden until the perfect time He wanted to release it. It will become a new well of revival where many will come up the mountain to this high place to encounter Him and His glory for generations to come.[2]

It is important to recognize that this breakthrough into a greater measure of my destiny happened in the context of the family of God in a *kairos* moment. I had a spiritual mother who prophesied this into being, a praying mortgage lender, a kindhearted real estate agent, a home group who prayed through every step, my family all behind me praying and supporting me, anointed saints who sowed into helping me cross the finish line, and confirmation wherever I turned. But I still had to take the first step.

I wonder if there might be more windows of opportunity available for us to lean into in this *kairos* moment as we move toward the slightest stirrings of the Holy Spirit. May this testimony inspire you to take that first step of faith toward Him where He is leading you today. Then watch as He opens wide the doors in front of you.

QUESTIONS FOR REFLECTION

Could this be the season, the *kairos* moment when things that were impossible in the past come together in perfect alignment for accelerated breakthrough? What window of opportunity is opening for you now? Who can you reach out to for prayer or to share your heart with?

CHAPTER 27

FINAL BREATH

We began the 2022–2023 School of Revival year with the powerful breakthrough where I was able to teach about the Apostolic Inheritance of California from my new Miracle House. We later dove into topics like the Jesus People Movement and Union with God. When the Asbury Revival broke out in February 2023, we shifted and did an intensive on that present-day move of God. A few of us even went there, inheriting new friends and spiritual family as a result. Usually, we finish the school year with a graduation and retreat at Carrie Judd Montgomery's Home of Peace in Oakland, California. Established in 1893, it is one of the first healing homes on the West Coast and a deep well of revival. But this year we decided to do something a little different. Instead of going to "re-dig" an existing well of revival, we decided to dig a new well of revival and all come to my Miracle House. We adjusted the dates of our retreat so one from our core team could make it, and we planned to end the year where we began: stepping into the Miracle House. This time it wouldn't just be me there alone, but my School of Revival family would be there as well.

Shortly before the retreat, I went with my mom and brother on her dream trip to Jordan in the Middle East. I came back early for our retreat while they continued their adventures for another week. When I got back home, I learned that my dad's health had declined. Before we left, he was doing well in his wheelchair and fully able to communicate.

When I got back, he was bedbound and struggled to eat or talk much. Over the next couple of days, he was aware and could hear everything, but his eyes stayed closed most of the time and he wasn't able to communicate verbally.

I saw him as much as I could the few days before our retreat. People were flying in from all over the nation to be together that Memorial Day weekend May 26–28, 2023. On Thursday of that week, I headed up the mountain to get the Miracle House ready and to have a little time with God in that sacred space. I drove back down the mountain Friday morning just to get a couple of hours with my dad before everyone arrived at the cabin later that day. Several of our School of Revival family came to visit my dad that morning on their way up. Every Friday at the assisted living home is a day to honor veterans, so they wear red. This Friday the staff dressed him in his red School of Revival t-shirt, which represents family to all of us. When the SOR family came, everyone was wearing their School of Revival t-shirts along with him. They got to sing over and pray for him, and then we all left to go up the mountain.

That night at Miracle House, we spent time in God's presence, laughing, eating, and enjoying being together. On Saturday we dove into the Scriptures, looking at 1 Kings 17 and how, when everything else is nearly lost, we need to hang on to our oil until the end. Then worship was released over the house, and we all just soaked in God's presence for a few hours. After lunch, some of us went on a hike to a place I like to call Declaration Rock, where you can see all the way to the beach on a clear day. That's when I got the call. My dad's breathing had changed. I knew right then I had to get there as soon as possible to be with him. My team leaders would have to facilitate the graduation and the rest of our end-of-year retreat by themselves.

We quickly walked back to the house. I gave hugs and asked everyone to pray that I would make it to see my dad before he passed. I threw my stuff in the car and then headed down the mountain. I have never been so focused on that drive to get there quickly and safely. I downloaded my dad's favorite song—"My Tribute (To God Be the Glory)" by Andraé Crouch—and listened to it at least ten times, crying and praying my heart out that I could make it there for him in time.

Thankfully, I made it to him in one piece. I didn't stop to sign in at the front desk but ran up the three flights of stairs to his room. He was in bed, breathing more irregularly than the day before, with oxygen tubes now in his nose. He was still wearing his red School of Revival t-shirt from the day before, and I happened to be wearing a matching purple one. Kim, one of the staff, stepped into the room a short time later. She was an angel sent from God to care for my father, and she loved him just as much as any of us did. She teared up when she saw me.

Though it felt peaceful in the room, I could see he was struggling and working hard to breathe. Hospice came and turned up his oxygen. Things shifted so quickly while I was there. At one point, hospice said he had two to three days and then, not long later, said he had only hours. I was prepared to stay all night and not leave his side. I played "To God Be the Glory" several times, and I know he heard it. I think I saw his foot move once, and he also raised his eyebrows a few times. Even though he couldn't sing out loud, his body tried its best to worship God in that moment.

As I sat next to him, holding his hand, I watched as my dad fought hard for each breath. It was painful to see him struggle, but I was grateful to be there. Thankfully, we were able to arrange a moment to FaceTime with my mom and brother still in the Middle East, so they could say goodbye. I was praying my dad's transition would be peaceful.

Several hours after he got to hear their voices, my dad's breathing shifted again. It transitioned from a fight to a release. He wasn't struggling for air anymore but was yielded. He began to breathe more slowly. Then, after several long pauses, he finally breathed his last and was so peacefully received into the arms of our heavenly Father. He didn't have to fight any longer. He was now with Jesus and had joined the cloud of witnesses. No more pain or suffering. He was free.

Through God's grace and Kim's foresight to call me, I was miraculously able to be by my dad's side for this transition. God had also prearranged for every other family member to be with relatives during the loss as well, and He made a way for each one to say their goodbyes beforehand. Only God. Though I was the only family member not there when my grandfather passed, I was the only family member with my dad when he transitioned into glory and breathed his last. It was another full-circle moment for me.

My dad went to heaven shortly after 10:00 p.m. on Saturday, May 27, 2023, which was also Pentecost weekend. I am so grateful God healed my dad when I was a newborn, so I could have the gift of his presence for so many years. Every day beyond that first miracle was a gift. My father's love and support laid the best foundation I could ever have for receiving the love of God the Father and having a healthy perspective of Him.

MIRACLE FLIGHT

The next day, on Pentecost Sunday, I woke up crying. As I read through my dad's Bible and places where he highlighted or wrote notes, I couldn't stop weeping all morning. After I had some time alone with the Lord to process and grieve a bit more, I invited the School of Revival family to come over for lunch at my mom's house where I was staying since they were all still in town. I was so thankful that God flew them all in to be with me during this defining weekend so I wouldn't be alone. They showered me with beautiful end-of-year gifts; we had lunch together and took communion together. In the aftermath of what I had experienced the night before, it was nice to have a house full of the spiritual family I had been running together with. They were incredibly supportive, praying, comforting, bringing joy, and helping with whatever needs my family and I had during that time. I needed to be with people who loved me in that moment and God provided so beautifully for this need.

At one point that afternoon while still at my mom's house where I grew up, I was showing a few of them my favorite bookshelf full of books written by the students who had taken my Writing in the Glory workshops. They also got to see the Welsh Revival chair from the 1903-04 revival in my room. Then I pulled out a copy of Carrie Judd Montgomery's 1880 *Prayer of Faith* book that she signed. I keep it in the envelope it came in, which also contains my miracle flight ticket. Several years back, I wanted to go to my friend's wedding in England, but I didn't have the money. I showed up at the San Francisco airport with my bags packed full of "testimonies" and with faith in a God who loves to love us. Long story short, at the airport the breakthrough came, and I got on a flight and made it to my friend's wedding in time. It was a miracle I will never forget, where I was surrounded by the family of Christ who encouraged me not to give up. In my book and ecourse on *Walking on Water*, I share my miracle flight story in-depth as well as on my blog.[1]

When we looked at the date of my miracle flight, it was May 28, 2014. The day we were all together in the house there was May 28, 2023. The ticket was for the exact day, just nine years before. At the time we discovered the ticket, it would have been the same time I would have been boarding that flight.

That day, I found myself in another defining moment. I had just lost my dad, the closest person I have ever had to lose, and God surrounded me with the beautiful body of Christ all flown in from different parts of the country to be with me during this transition. He knew when we changed dates and location for the retreat what I would need in that precise moment and He so faithfully provided. He was reminding me that His ways and His timing are orchestrated by heaven.

My dad transitioned into glory on Pentecost weekend. If you know me, you know how much of my life I have given to the story of Pentecost in Acts 2 and the Azusa Street Revival testimony inspired by it. The day after he passed was also the anniversary of my miracle flight. The miracle flight was a marking time in my life, just like this Pentecost weekend was becoming. Just as it was with the miracle flight, with my dad's transition I felt I was beginning a new vulnerable journey where I needed my spiritual family to carry me once again. I am so grateful for the beautiful body of Christ and how Jesus is coming back for a pure, spotless bride.

I am writing this chapter just days after my father's passing. I can't tell you how important it is to surround yourself with family, both natural and spiritual. We need each other on this journey called life. We were never made to go on this journey alone. He has given us the gifts of each other, especially for times like these. May He release His comforting love in all spaces of pain and pour out His healing presence in your life. May you receive an impartation of the Father's great love and His grace demonstrated through His beloved bride, the body of Christ. Selah.

QUESTIONS FOR REFLECTION

Thinking back, are there any special moments in your life when God poured out His love to you through the body of Christ? How has He used your spiritual family to demonstrate His comfort, encouragement, and provision over the years? How can you thank God and those He has brought to help you in your times of need for their generosity and love?

CHAPTER 28

TAKE THE FIRST STEP

I absolutely believe we are in a *kairos* moment. We are in a special time where things are being accelerated like never before. There is an open window in front of us right now.

Each one of us has been perfectly positioned for such a time as this. God is not surprised by the passing of my father, the crisis you just had to walk through or are currently in, the global pandemic, the effects of the lockdown, the political swirl, the racial divides, the refugee crisis, the war in Ukraine, and more. He determined the times we would live in. No other generation has been given the opportunity to steward a moment in history like we have today. In this time of deep turmoil, there is an invitation for revival and reformation. There is a clean slate set before us. We get to decide today what we want the world to look like on the other side of these challenges. What will we do with what God has put in our hands and entrusted us with?

In this time of increasing darkness, He has called us to blaze a trail of light. And He has called us to do it *together*. There will always be a *before* and an *after* the 2020 pandemic. The way we do church and family after the pandemic must look radically different than it did before, or we will have missed out on the reformation fire meant to purify and realign us. We need a new normal that prioritizes family as the fireplace of revival above religious systems and structures.

Because the revival we've been praying for our whole lives is imminently upon us, and is already here, there is a need to position ourselves to steward this next great awakening well. We can do this only with and in family. We don't have much more time to prepare our nets before they will be bursting at the seams, beyond full capacity.

No matter what your past looks like, no matter the failures you've experienced, or the regrets and mistakes, I want to share good news with you. Today is a new day! It's a new era where anything and everything is possible. For those of you who have felt sidelined by the enemy's lies because of things in your past, I want to call you back into your rightful place and position in the kingdom of God.

The harvest is ripe. You are needed as a spiritual mother or father to help steward this incoming harvest. You are no longer an orphan. You are a son. You are a daughter of the King. You belong in the family of God. He is calling you who have been sidelined in the past to step up and onto the front lines where you belong. He has wiped away the shame, forgiven you, and He needs you to take your place.

Your past cannot define you or disqualify you anymore from what God is calling you into in this *kairos* moment. There is nothing that can exclude you from the love and redemptive power of Jesus Christ today. God has already covered your past. In Psalm 139:4–5 (TPT), David says to God, "You know every step I will take before my journey even begins. You've gone into my future to prepare the way, and in kindness you follow behind me to spare me from the harm of my past." God is not only watching your back, but He has also gone before you to prepare your next step.

It's time to come off the sidelines and step onto the front lines.

You were born for such a time as this. This world needs you to return to the front lines where you belong. People's lives are depending upon your one "yes." The only thing God requires from you is a simple act of obedience.

If you haven't found or taken your place yet, find it in Him. Find it in family. God is on the front lines. He is calling other burning ones to line up and take their rightful place alongside you.[1]

It's time to throw off everything that hinders from the past. It's time to take that first step toward the things God has put in your heart so that you can then *run* the race He has set before *you*. Fix your eyes on JESUS, the Author, Pioneer, and Perfecter of your faith, He will never let you down.

> *Therefore, since we are surrounded by such a great cloud of witnesses, let us throw off everything that hinders and the sin that so easily entangles. And let us run with perseverance the race marked out for us, fixing our eyes on Jesus, the pioneer and perfecter of faith. For the joy set before him he endured the cross, scorning its shame, and sat down at the right hand of the throne of God.*
>
> Hebrews 12:1–2

It's time to RUN, my friends.

And to do it together with a family of burning ones.

We have decided to follow Jesus . . .

No turning back.

No turning back.[2]

COMMISSIONING

by Heidi Baker

God is calling us today to a place of utter surrender, where we hold nothing of ourselves back from the waters of baptism. He would have all of us submerged so that we may come to live in a place of constant intimacy. We must not be afraid to take the low and humble path. The river of life flows down, even to the lowest places of the earth. As we remain in Him, we can also soar as high as the Spirit takes us. High or low, in our hearts we can always remain with Him. There is no greater joy.

In the natural and in the spiritual, there is much more shaking to come in this world. But I truly believe it is the Church's greatest time to shine. In Him we have every necessary provision. This is a time for those who know who they are in Christ to reach out in His endless love toward the broken, the sick, the dying, and the lost. This is a time to give of ourselves, from the heart. It is not a time for fear. It is a time for trust.

I believe that the time Jesus spoke of is truly at hand: "I tell you, open your eyes and look at the fields! They are ripe for harvest" (John 4:35).

APPENDIX

RELATIONSHIP ALIGNMENT EXERCISE

This is an exercise to help bring greater clarity, focus, and alignment for you to steward key kingdom relationships the Lord is entrusting you with in this season. There are times when we are looking to answer the "What?" question when God might be trying to get us to answer the "Who?" question first. He loves to birth beautiful things from a place of overflow in kingdom relationships.

I do this exercise several times a year to make sure that I am intentionally investing in the key relationships God is leading me to in each season. One time I was at a stadium revival event in Germany and I realized I had two people from each category that were also there at the same time.[1] Recognizing that encouraged me that I was being purposeful in running together with those who God had called me to partner with in that season. Now it's your turn.

1. Write down one word or theme you feel God is leading you into or defines your present season (Healing, Restoration, Family, Preparation, Acceleration, Revival, Rest, Intimacy, etc.).

2. Next, think about who else in your life is also passionate about this same thing or in a similar season? Ask the Holy Spirit to highlight four spiritual mothers or fathers (these could be mentors, advisors, coaches, etc.), four peers or friends, and four spiritual sons or daughters, or people

to mentor and disciple in this season who also burn for the same thing that you do right now.

Mentors/Spiritual Mothers & Fathers

1. _____

2. _____

3. _____

4. _____

Friends/Peers

1. _____

2. _____

3. _____

4. _____

People to Mentor/Disciple

1. _____

2. _____

3. _____

4. _____

This list will regularly change in various seasons of your life. Some people will remain solid rocks and constants in your life over the long term, while others may shift in different seasons. There is nothing wrong with the ebb and flow in relationship if the Holy Spirit is bringing transition and re-alignment. As we grow, many times our relationships must also grow or shift. Many times God will bring people into our lives for a season and other times there will be a more long-term relationship that continues with us on our journey for decades. We must recognize each of these relationships as gifts from God and be grateful to Him and to the person for the blessing of their friendship for however long or short they are in our lives (James 1:17).

It's also important to point out that just because someone isn't on your list right now doesn't mean they are not significant in your life. It is still important to make time for the people that matter to you even if they don't share your same passion in this season. Additionally, it's important to look for those kindred spirits you can strategically run together with after the things of God.

Now that you have your list that the Holy Spirit has highlighted for you in this season, pray over each one of them, and try to be more intentional in sharing your heart and prioritizing time with these. Ask the Holy Spirit to lead you in creative ways to deepen these connections. Then watch and see what fruit will come. Don't be discouraged if some people who were highlighted to you do no reciprocate. It may just be for another time. Move on and ask God to bring to mind another person who might be more available or feel the same way in this season to fill that gap. As you are intentional in building kingdom relationships, watch what God will do.

You can also welcome a baptism of fire over your relationships. If you are ready for change and alignment in this area, I encourage you to pray this prayer inspired by John 15 out loud today:

> *Jesus, You are my Best Friend and the One who meets all my needs. Forgive me for any time I have run to other lovers before You. I repent of any idolatry and I enthrone*

You alone as Lord of my Life. I choose to run to You as my Source always. Every good and perfect gift comes from You, the Father of lights. You are the Alpha and the Omega, the Beginning and the End of all things, even of my relationships.

God, I come before You now and lay every relationship down at the altar. Pour Your oil over each one and send Your refining fire. I surrender all to You. I give You permission to burn away any relationships that don't bring You glory or that no longer belong in my life in this season. Remove, refine, readjust, restore, or realign the connections in my life to be in correct kingdom order. If You are taking someone away, I trust that it's for my best interest and that You are making space to bring something better. Thank You Father for each friend You have gifted me with in previous seasons. I choose to let go, bless, release, and entrust each one to You.

Thank You for those friendships You have blessed me with now, and those You will add in Your timing. Refine, strengthen, and deepen the relationships that You want to remain. In the fire of Your burning love, let the gold rise to the surface. Surround me with other kindred-spirit Jesus lovers who are on fire for You. Plant me in a healthy spiritual family that receives me for the gift that I am and where I will grow. For any new kingdom relationships You want to add, lead us by Your Spirit to find each other. Bring divine appointments. Teach me how to be a loving friend to all You bring.

Pour out Your Spirit in increasing measures upon my relationships. Give me courage to open wide my heart in vulnerability as I learn to go deeper with You and the others

You are gifting me with in this season. I declare alignment with heaven over each of my friendships and ask that Your glory would fall upon us as we seek Your face. Let beautiful things be birthed as we grow together in You. Thank You for the spiritual family You have ordained and orchestrated for me to be a part of in this kairos *moment. Cover each of these relationships with Your protection. In Jesus' name, amen and let it be so.*

*This exercise is influenced and adapted from the activation found in Jennifer A. Miskov, *Walking on Water: Experiencing a Life of Miracles, Courageous Faith, and Union with God* (Bloomington, MN: Chosen, 2017), 96-98.

Other helpful resources along these lines of growing in relational discernment and building spiritual family are:

- *Relational Intelligence: The People Skills you Need for the Life of Purpose You Want* by Dharius Daniels (Grand Rapids, MI: Zondervan, 2020).

- *Safe People: How to Find Relationships that Are Good for You and Avoid Those that Aren't and Boundaries: When to Say Yes, How to Say No to Take Control of Your Life* by Henry Cloud and John Townsend (Grand Rapids, MI: Zondervan).

- *Fire on the Family Altar: Experience the Holy Spirit's Power in Your Home* by Cheryl Sacks (Shippensburg, PA: Destiny Image, 2023). This is more specifically in relation to your natural family.

- *Developing the Leader Within You, Developing the Leaders Around You, The Self-Aware Leader,* and anything by John

C. Maxwell will be helpful in relation to leadership and building relationships with teams.

- *A Life that Really Matters: The Story of the John Wesley Great Experiment,* by Danny E. Morris (Franklin, TN: Providence House Publishers, 1965 and 1999) for those who want some help to intentionally grow with those God has highlighted.

- School of Revival modules: Family Is the Fireplace of Revival, Walking on Water, Fasting for Fire, Holy Spirit, Martyrdom, and more. Consider gathering with some of the ones God has highlighted or forming a small group of burning ones to go through a School of Revival online module together. This will accelerate your spiritual growth in the area of surrender, revival fire, and intimacy with God and the family of God.[2]

CORE VALUES ACTIVATION

It is important we know where we are going in life. Proverbs 29:18 (ISV) says, "Without prophetic vision, people abandon restraint, but those who obey the Law are happy." Vision helps to set the plumb line to make sure we are aligned and going in the direction of our God-given purpose. Core values help solidify and build the vision God has given us to make sure we stay true to ourselves and walk with integrity toward the things He has entrusted us with. Below are the vision statements and core values of two ministries I was a part of birthing. The core values were shaped and formed in the process of running after God together and yielding to the leading of the Holy Spirit.

DESTINY HOUSE (2012–2019)

Our *vision* was to cultivate revival in family so that from a place of intimacy with Jesus and connection to the body of Christ, people were launched into a greater measure of their destinies.

The following core values were developed during our experience at Destiny House along with some of the practical ways we lived these out in our unique context.

Glory: We seek to worship God in all circumstances (2 Chronicles 20) and to host His presence well. We believe that the keys to our destiny are released through intimacy with Jesus and through connection with the body of Christ. One way we live out this core value is by **hosting a weekly worship encounter time** together as family (Friday mornings), where the only agenda is to adore Jesus together (Psalm 27).

Honor: We seek to honor God, each other, and the ones He brings to us. We want to grow in deeper connection with our tribe by intentionally sharing life together (whether living in the same house or not). One way we live this out is by **sharing a meal together** at least once a week (Monday nights) and gathering for the purpose of knowing, being known, and encouraging each other (Acts 2). The key is to create a safe place to be vulnerable, minister to one another, and be fully present.

Destiny: We seek to create space for and empower each one to fulfill their God-given destinies as well as steward the power of the testimony. We believe that as we abide in God's presence and grow closer to each other, the keys of our destiny are released (Ephesians 3:14–21). When this happens, people naturally step into a greater measure of their destiny. One way we live this out is by creating space to **activate people** during our weekly worship gatherings, where they are launched in preaching, leading worship, dance, prophesying, hospitality, healing, creative expressions, or other things they are passionate about.

Consecration: We seek to burn for Jesus with wholehearted surrender and yieldedness to Him. We believe that like the Levite tribe of worshipers, we are called to steward the fire in our hearts and keep it burning day and night (Leviticus 6:8–13). We are called to remain full of the oil (Matthew 25:1–13). One way we live this out is by cultivating a rhythm of **fasting and feasting** together as a community (on Mondays), as well as stewarding the Sabbath rest.

Our culture was shaped and informed by our core values and naturally included the following elements.

Creativity: We believe that everyone is a gift to this world and that they have something special to share. We seek to facilitate environments where people can express their creativity in their specific and unique ways (Ephesians 2:10).

Risk Taking: We believe that in the process of taking risks toward stepping out in faith and following their hearts, people are awakened to become more of the person they are created to be. The word *failure* does not exist here (Romans 8:28).

Integrity: We seek to model and integrate people into our team who have high levels of integrity, those who are willing to pay a price to stay true to themselves and their convictions. Integrity is proved over time as people stay committed to a common vision. The original meaning of the word *passion* comes from the same word as *suffering*. We are not afraid to pay a price for what we believe in.

SCHOOL OF REVIVAL (2020–PRESENT)

The core values of School of Revival were built off the foundations of what I had learned and experienced while leading Destiny House and take on similar themes.

We define our **vision** and culture this way: We seek to partner with the Holy Spirit to ignite revival from a place of overflow from our relationship with God and each other. We cultivate family around the presence and fire of God. **By integrating revival history with present-day revivalists,** we cultivate **revival in family** by bringing together fiery revivalists from around the globe to burn together for more of Jesus in our online School of Revival intensives, in-person meetings, retreat, and through our other trainings and resources. **We believe that family is the fireplace of revival, which is reflected in our core values below.**

Family: This consists of honor, vulnerability, creativity, and destiny.

Fire: This consists of intimacy, focus, consecration, and the fire of the Holy Spirit.

Revival: This consists of the power of the testimony, God's presence, pioneering revival, and stewarding the harvest.

As you can see, there are common threads between both Destiny House and School of Revival because both reflect some of my personal core values. What is important to you will impact and become important to the people you lead.

ACTIVATION

What is your life vision or purpose statement? What are you born for? What kind of impact or contribution do you feel called to make in this generation?

If you are leading a team or a ministry, what is the vision statement for that community?

Which core values stood out the most to you and why? What other core values has God formed within you?

Write out three of your top core values that align with your life vision. Then below each one, write why that core value is important to you, as well as what it looks like lived out in your context. It can also be beneficial to do this together with a core team who God has brought alongside you to help you build in this season.

Top 3 Core Values

1. _____

2. _____

3. _____

What these 3 Core Values practically look like lived out

1. _____

2. _____

3. _____

*For more information on Destiny House core values go to JenMiskov.com/vision-core-values.

For more information on School of Revival core values go to SchoolofRevivalFire.com.

NOTES

EPIGRAPH

1. Lit. A mighty flame of the Lord (Yah, poetic form of YHWH)

CHAPTER 1: DIVING IN

1. See Jennifer A. Miskov, "There's a Tidal Wave of Revival on the Horizon," *Charisma Magazine* online (February 17, 2014), https://www.charismanews.com/opinion/42887-there-s-a -tidal-wave-of-revival-on-the-horizon.

2. Much of this paragraph is based off a section called "Momentum" in Jennifer A. Miskov, *Ignite Azusa: Positioning for a New Jesus Revolution* (Redding, CA: Silver to Gold, 2016), 85. Used with permission by Jennifer A. Miskov.

3. See Matthew 25:1–13; Colossians 3:13; Ephesians 4:32; Matthew 5:23–34; John 15:17.

4. See Philippians 1:29; 2 Timothy 3:12; Matthew 5:10; Mark 10:29–30.

5. See Psalm 133; Matthew 18:19–20; Ephesians 2:19–22.

6. Frank Bartleman wrote this in June 1906, just a few months
   after the Azusa Street Revival was catalyzed. See Frank
   Bartleman, *How Pentecost Came to Los Angeles: As It Was in
   the Beginning,* 2nd edition (Los Angeles, CA: Frank Bartleman,
   originally April 1925), 65. Now printed by Christian Classic
   Ethereal Library (Grand Rapids, MI), accessed January 25,
   2016, http://www.ccel.org/ccel/bartleman/los.pdf.

CHAPTER 2: SURF LESSONS

1. To learn more about my trip and to see pictures and a video, go
   to https://jenmiskov.com/blog//monastery-adventures.

CHAPTER 3: *KAIROS*

1. Strong's G2540. https://www.blueletterbible.org/lang/
   lexicon/lexicon.cfm?Strongs=G2540&t=KJV. See Ephesians
   5:15–16 for an example of the word *kairos.*

2. These are the Scriptures that have the word *kairos* used in
   them, along with a few Old Testament verses they stem
   from: Genesis 1:14; 2 Chronicles 8:13; Daniel 2:21; 7:25;
   12:7; Matthew 8:29; 11:25; 12:1; 13:30; 14:1; 16:3; 21:34;
   21:41; 24:45; 26:18; Mark 1:15; 10:30; 11:13; 12:2; 13:33;
   Luke 1:20; 4:13; 8:13; 12:42; 12:56; 13:1, 16; 18:30; 19:44;
   20:10; 21:8; 21:24, 36; John 5:4; 7:6, 8; Acts 1:7; 3:20; 7:20;
   12:1; 13:11; 14:17; 17:26; 19:23; 24:25; Romans 3:26; 5:6;
   8:18; 9:9; 11:5; 12:11; 13:11; 1 Corinthians 4:5; 7:5, 29; 2
   Corinthians 6:2; 8:14; Galatians 4:10; 6:9–10; Ephesians
   1:10; 2:12; 5:16; 6:18; Colossians 4:5; 1 Thessalonians 2:17;
   5:1; 2 Thessalonians 2:6; 1 Timothy 2:6; 4:1; 6:15; 2 Timothy

3:1; 4:3, 6; Titus 1:3; Hebrews 9:9–10; 11:11, 15; 1 Peter 1:5; 1:11; 4:17; 5:6; Revelation 1:3; 11:18; 12:12, 14; 22:10. "And do this, understanding the present time *[kairos]*: The hour has already come for you to wake up from your slumber, because our salvation is nearer now than when we first believed" (Romans 13:11). "Therefore judge nothing before the appointed time *[kairos]*; wait until the Lord comes. He will bring to light what is hidden in darkness and will expose the motives of the heart. At that time each will receive their praise from God" (1 Corinthians 4:5). "And pray in the Spirit on all occasions *[kairos]* with all kinds of prayers and requests. With this in mind, be alert and always keep on praying for all the Lord's people" (Ephesians 6:18). "Hypocrites! You know how to interpret the appearance of the earth and the sky. How is it that you don't know how to interpret this present time *[kairos]*? (Luke 12:56). "But keep on the alert at all times *[kairos]*, praying that you may have strength to escape all these things that are about to take place, and to stand before the Son of Man" (Luke 21:36 NASB). "From time to time *[kairos]* an angel of the Lord would come down and stir up the waters. The first one into the pool after each such disturbance would be cured of whatever disease they had" (John 5:4). "Yet he has not left himself without testimony: He has shown kindness by giving you rain from heaven and crops in their seasons *[kairos]*; he provides you with plenty of food and fills your hearts with joy" (Acts 14:17). "For I am already being poured out like a drink offering, and the time *[kairos]* for my departure is near" (2 Timothy 4:6).

3. See Acts 7:20; Esther 4:14.

4. One of the words used for "harvest" in the Greek is *therismos*, which means "harvest" or "the act of reaping." There is also

another word used for harvest *(karpos)*, which means "fruit" and is used 66 times in 56 verses. It is interesting to see this word paired with *kairos* in the following verses: "When the harvest *[karpos]* time *[kairos]* approached, he sent his servants to the tenants to collect his fruit *[karpos]*" (Matthew 21:34). "At harvest time *[kairos]* he sent a servant to the tenants so they would give him some of the fruit *[karpos]* of the vineyard. But the tenants beat him and sent him away empty-handed" (Luke 20:10). "At the harvest time *[kairos]* he sent a slave to the vine-growers, in order to receive some of the produce *[karpos]* of the vineyard from the vine-growers" (Mark 12:2 NASB). Strong's G2326. https://www.blueletterbible.org/lang/lexicon/lexicon.cfm?Strongs=G2326&t=NIV.

5. See my first book, *Silver to Gold: A Journey of Young Revolutionaries* (Birmingham, England: Silver to Gold, 2009), which is an allegory about this exact story.

6. Additionally, I introduce "sacred time" into this discussion as a "special season when revivals, awakenings, and stirrings of the Holy Spirit are concentrated and occur in higher frequency than in other times... when people all around the world experience heightened manifestations of God's presence" at the same time. Jennifer A. Miskov, "Coloring Outside the Lines: Pentecostal Parallels with Expressionism. The Work of the Spirit in Place, Time, and Secular Society?", *Journal of Pentecostal Theology* 19 (2010), 115.

7. To read about my time at Asbury and see pictures and videos from my time there, go to https://jenmiskov.com/blog/asburyrevival2023.

CHAPTER 4: ESTABLISHING CULTURE

1. Miskov, *Ignite Azusa,* 85–90.

2. Miskov, *Ignite Azusa,* 85–90.

3. "Creating a Culture to Steward the Billion-Soul Harvest" in Miskov, *Ignite Azusa,* 85–90. Used with permission by Jennifer A. Miskov.

4. Unknown author, "Beginning of World Wide Revival," *The Apostolic Faith 1:5* (312 Azusa Street, Los Angeles, CA: January, 1907), 1. "From the little mustard seed faith that was given to a little company of people waiting on God in a cottage prayer meeting, a great tree has grown, so that people from all parts of the country are coming like birds to lodge in the branches thereof. (Matt. 13:31- 32.) The faith is still growing, and we are still just in the beginning, earnestly contending for the faith once delivered unto the saints."

5. This section is taken directly from chapter 9: "Preparing to Steward the Next Great Awakening" in Jennifer A. Miskov, *Ignite Azusa,* 85–90. This comes after sections about the power of the testimony, the billion-soul harvest prophecies, and the Azusa Street Revival story.

6. John Wesley and John Emory, *The Works of the Reverend John Wesley* (New York: T. Mason and G. Lane for the Methodist Episcopal Church, 1831), 156.

CHAPTER 6: FIRE

1. See Jennifer A. Miskov, *Fasting for Fire: Igniting Fresh Hunger to Feast Upon God* (Shippensburg, PA: Destiny Image, 2021) for more about significance and root words connected to fire.

2. Smith Wigglesworth, "The Substance of Things Hoped For." *Pentecostal Evangel,* October 25, 1924, in *Smith Wigglesworth: The Complete Collection of His Life Teachings,* comp. Roberts Liardon (New Kensington, PA: Whitaker House, 1996), 464–465.

3. Read Miskov, *Fasting for Fire,* for more about fasting for the fire.

4. http://www.etymonline.com/index.php?term=focus "Taken by Kepler (1604) in a mathematical sense for 'point of convergence,' perhaps on analogy of the burning point of a lens." See also synonyms: center, heart, core, nucleus, point of convergence (http://www.thesaurus.com/browse/focus).

5. Jennifer A. Miskov, *Walking on Water: Experiencing a Life of Miracles, Courageous Faith & Union with God* (Bloomington, MN: Chosen Books, 2017). 72–73. See also www.merriam -webster.com/dictionary/hearth.

CHAPTER 7: REVIVAL

1. Strong's H2421: "to live, whether literally or figuratively; causatively, to revive:—keep (leave, make) alive, certainly, give (promise) life, (let, suffer to) live, nourish up, preserve (alive), quicken, recover, repair, restore (to life), revive, (God) save

(alive, life, lives), surely, be whole." https://www
.blueletterbible.org/lexicon/h2421/nkjv/wlc/0-1.

2. "But when they told him all the words which Joseph had said
   to them, and when he saw the carts which Joseph had sent to
   carry him, the spirit of Jacob their father *revived*" (Genesis
   45:27 NKJV).

3. "Then the LORD heard the voice of Elijah; and the soul of
   the child came back to him, and he *revived*" (1 Kings 17:22
   NKJV).

4. "So it was, as they were burying a man, that suddenly they
   spied a band of raiders; and they put the man in the tomb of
   Elisha; and when the man was let down and touched the bones
   of Elisha, he *revived* and stood on his feet" (2 Kings 13:21).

5. Psalm 71:20 is a call to be delivered from great troubles. Psalm
   80:18 is a reviving in order to turn back to God.

   Psalm 85:6 says, "Will You not *revive* us again, that Your
   people may rejoice in You?" There is purpose to praise in the
   reviving work. We see in Psalm 119:25, 107, and 154 that one
   can be *revived according to His word*: "*Revive* me according
   to Your word" (119:25 NKJV). According to Psalm 119:37
   (NKJV), we can be *revived in His way*: "Turn away my eyes
   from looking at worthless things, and *revive* me in Your
   way." In Psalm 119:40 (NKJV), we can be *revived in His
   righteousness*: "Behold, I long for Your precepts; *revive* me
   in Your righteousness." Psalm 119:88 and 159 say we can be
   revived according to His lovingkindness: "*Revive* me according
   to Your lovingkindness, so that I may keep the testimony
   of Your mouth" (Psalm 119:88 NKJV). In Psalm 119:149
   (NKJV), we can be *revived according to His justice*: "Hear my
   voice according to Your lovingkindness; O LORD, *revive* me

according to Your justice." Psalm 119:156 (NKJV) says we can be *revived according to His judgments.* "Great are Your tender mercies, O LORD; *revive* me according to Your judgments." In Psalm 138:7, *when in trouble* we can be revived: "Though I walk in the midst of trouble, You will *revive* me; You will stretch out Your hand against the wrath of my enemies, and Your right hand will save me" (NASB). In Psalm 143:11, we can be *revived for His name's sake:* "Revive me, O LORD, for Your name's sake! For Your righteousness' sake bring my soul out of trouble" (NKJV).

6. Isaiah 57:15 says, "For thus says the High and Lofty One, who inhabits eternity, whose name is Holy: 'I dwell in the high and holy place, with him who has a contrite and humble spirit, to *revive* the spirit of the humble, and to *revive* the heart of the contrite ones'" (NKJV). And then in Habakkuk 3:2: "O LORD, I have heard Your speech and was afraid; O LORD, *revive* Your work in the midst of the years! In the midst of the years make it known; in wrath remember mercy" (NKJV).

7. https://www.etymonline.com/word/revival.

8. According to the Merriam-Webster Dictionary, the word *revival* can mean: "1: an act or instance of reviving: the state of being revived: such as a: renewed attention to or interest in something b: a new presentation or publication of something old c (1): a period of renewed religious interest (2): an often highly emotional evangelistic meeting or series of meetings 2: restoration of force, validity, or effect (as to a contract)." Accessed December 11, 2022, https://www.merriam-webster .com/dictionary/revival.

9. https://www.merriam-webster.com/dictionary/revival.

10. Collin Hansen and John Woodbridge, *A God-Sized Vision: Revival Stories that Stretch and Stir* (Grand Rapids, MI: Zondervan, 2010), 31.

11. https://www.etymonline.com/word/revival.

12. Roger Finke and Rodney Stark, *The Churching of America 1776–1990: Winners and Losers in Our Religious Economy* (New Brunswick: Rutgers University Press, 1992), 92. According to Finke and Stark, while "all organizations need renewals or revivals of member commitment, it is also true that these must be episodic. People can't stay excited indefinitely." Most people don't have the capacity to remain in a heightened state of being revived.

13. Charles G. Finney, *Lectures of Revivals on Religion* (New York, NY: Fleming H. Revell Company, 1868), 14. https://www.ccel.org/ccel/f/finney/revivals/cache/revivals.pdf.

14. "There is so little principle in the church, so little firmness and stability of purpose, that unless the religious feelings are awakened and kept excited, counter worldly feeling and excitement will prevail, and men will not obey God. They have so little knowledge, and their principles are so weak, that unless they are excited, they will go back from the path of duty, and do nothing to promote the glory of God. The state of the world is still such, and probably will be till the millennium is fully come, that religion must be mainly promoted by means of revivals. How long and how often has the experiment been tried, to bring the church to act steadily for God, without these periodical excitements. Many good men have supposed, and still suppose, that the best way to promote religion, is to go along uniformly, and gather in the ungodly gradually, and without excitement. But however sound such reasoning

may appear in the abstract, facts demonstrate its futility. If the church were far enough advanced in knowledge, and had stability of principle enough to keep awake, such a course would do; but the church is so little enlightened, and there are so many counteracting causes, that she will not go steadily to work without a special interest being awakened.

"As the millennium advances, it is probable that these periodical excitements will be unknown. Then the church will be enlightened, and the counteracting causes removed, and the entire church will be in a state of habitual and steady obedience to God." Finney, *Lectures of Revivals on Religion*, 9.

15. Finney, *Lectures of Revivals on Religion*, 12.

16. Martin Lloyd-Jones, *Revival* (Wheaton, IL: Crossway, 1987), 199, in Hansen and Woodbridge, *A God-Sized Vision*, 35.

17. Elmer Towns and Douglas Porter, *The Ten Greatest Revivals Ever: From Pentecost to Present* (Ann Arbor, MI: Servant Publications, 2000), 133 and accessed https://digitalcommons.liberty.edu/cgi/viewcontent.cgi?article=1192&context=towns_books.

18. Duncan Campbell, *The Price and Power of Revival,* (reprint by Solid Christian Books, 2015), 45.

19. William Faupel, "The Everlasting Gospel: The Significance of Eschatology in the Development of Pentecostal Thought," *Journal of Pentecostal Theology Supplement Series,* ed. John Christopher Thomas, Rickie D. Moore, and Steven J. Land, vol. 10. (Sheffield: Sheffield Academic Press, 1996).

20. Mark Stibbe, *Revival, The Thinking Clear Series,* ed. Clive Calver (London: Monarch Books, 1998), 14, 223.

21. Stibbe, *Revival,* 17.

22. Stibbe, *Revival,* 49.

23. Miskov, "Coloring Outside the Lines," 94–117.

Chapter 8: Just the Beginning

1. Rolland Baker, *Keeping the Fire: Sustaining Revival Through Love: The Five Core Values of Iris Global* (Kent, United Kingdom: River Publishing & Media Ltd, 2015), 141–143. Used with permission in an email dated 12/19/2022 from Tim Pettingale, director of River Publishing & Media Ltd.

2. Hansen and Woodbridge, *A God-Sized Vision,* 25.

Chapter 9: Waiting for the Fire

1. https://www.blueletterbible.org/lang/lexicon/lexicon.cfm?strongs=G3306&t=KJV.

2. https://www.blueletterbible.org/lang/lexicon/lexicon.cfm?Strongs=G2842&t=NIV.

Part 3: Moravian Legacy

1. To see pictures and read more about this time in Germany, go to https://jenmiskov.com/blog//inheritance-in-germany-january-2018.

Chapter 10: The Invisible Body

1. J. E. Hutton M.A., *A History of the Moravian Church* (second edition, revised and enlarged) (London: Moravian Publication Office 32 Fetter Lane, 1909), 177.

2. Hutton, *A History of the Moravian Church*, 178.

3. Hutton, *A History of the Moravian Church*, 182.

4. Hutton, *A History of the Moravian Church*, 182–183.

5. Hutton, *A History of the Moravian Church*, 185.

6. Hutton, *A History of the Moravian Church*, 187.

7. Hutton, *A History of the Moravian Church*, 188–189.

Chapter 11: Moravian Pentecost

1. Hutton, *A History of the Moravian Church*, 397.

2. Hutton, *A History of the Moravian Church*, 209.

3. Hutton, *A History of the Moravian Church*, 209–210.

4. Hutton, *A History of the Moravian Church*, 211.

5. Hutton, *A History of the Moravian Church*, 211.

6. Hutton, *A History of the Moravian Church*, 221.

Chapter 12: Radical Missions

1. Hutton, *A History of the Moravian Church*, 234.

2. Hutton, *A History of the Moravian Church*, 234.

3. Hutton, *A History of the Moravian Church*, 236.

4. Hutton, *A History of the Moravian Church*, 237.

5. Hutton, *A History of the Moravian Church*, 239.

6. The Moravians understood the significance of prayer covering and kingdom partnerships. While the missionaries were on the front lines, those at homebase were faithful to steward the furnace of intercession to cover them on the field. In Exodus 17:8–13, we see the powerful partnership of Moses sending Joshua onto the front lines. He didn't just send him there and then forget about him. He stood on top of the hill and labored with him for victory. Whenever Moses' hands were raised, Joshua would have success. Whenever they fell, Joshua would start to be defeated. When Moses' hands grew tired, Aaron and Hur held them up. They kept his hands raised until sunset, so Joshua could overcome the enemy. Multiple people were involved in the victory, both on the front lines and behind the scenes. If we liken Moses sending Joshua to the front lines to a church sending a missionary to the field, we can see there is a vital need for the home church to contend on behalf of the one sent out. The Moravians teach us that just because we are not on the front lines doesn't mean we don't have an important role to play in care and intercession.

CHAPTER 13: PEACE IN THE STORM

1. Percy Livingstone Parker, ed., *The Heart of John Wesley's Journal* (London: Fleming H. Revell Company, 1903),

xxxiil. Accessible online at https://openlibrary.org/works/ OL996945W/The_journal_of_the_Rev._John_Wesley.

2. John Wesley, *The Works of the Rev. John Wesley,* A.M., Volume 1:11 (London: John Mason, 14 City-road, 1856), 21.

3. Wesley, *The Works of the Rev. John Wesley,* 22.

4. Wesley, *The Works of the Rev. John Wesley,* 24.

5. Wesley, *The Works of the Rev. John Wesley,* 24.

6. Bill Johnson with Jennifer A. Miskov, *Defining Moments: God Encounters with Ordinary People Who Changed the World* (New Kensington, PA: Whitaker House, 2016), 20–21.

7. Parker, ed., *The Heart of John Wesley's Journal,* 42–45.

CHAPTER 14: RIPPLE EFFECTS

1. Wesley, *The Works of the Rev. John Wesley,* 100.

2. Ernest Rhys, ed., *The Journal of the Rev. John Wesley in Everyman's Library,* vol. 1 (London: J.M. Dent & Sons Limited, London, 1906), 169. https://babel.hathitrust.org/ cgi/pt?id=mdp.39015041157986.

3. Johnson and Miskov, *Defining Moments,* 29.

CHAPTER 15: DIGGING THE WELLS OF REVIVAL

1. Many of these trips, along with other testimonies shared throughout this book can also be found more in-depth with pictures on my blog at https://jenmiskov.com/blog-posts.

2. To see pictures and learn more about my trip here https:// jenmiskov.com/blog/2015/07/16/moravians.

3. To see pictures and videos, and to learn more about my trip, go here https://jenmiskov.com/blog//england-czech-republic -mozambique-recap-2018.

4. To see pictures and read testimonies of my trips and other adventures, go to https://jenmiskov.com/blog-posts.

CHAPTER 17: STEWARDSHIP

1. To learn more about this story, go to https://jenmiskov.com/ blog/2013/02/10/201329defeating-armies-by-praise.

CHAPTER 18: MARTYRDOM

1. To read more of this account and see photos from the night, go to https://jenmiskov.com/blog/runtothealtar.

CHAPTER 19: TOGETHER

1. See Deuteronomy 32:30 and Ecclesiastes 4:9–12.

2. Maria Woodworth-Etter, *Acts of the Holy Ghost, or The Life, Work, and Experience of Mrs. M.B. Woodworth-Etter Evangelist* (Dallas, TX: John F. Worley Printing Co., 1912), 42–43. In the middle of this text, she said, "I was a little frightened, as I did not know what the people would think or what they might do to me, as I was the leader of the meeting. While the fear of God was on the people, and I was looking on, not knowing

what to do, the Spirit of God brought before me the vision
I had before I started out in the work of the Lord, and said:
'Don't you remember when you was [sic] carried away, and saw
a field of wheat and the sheaves falling? The large field of wheat
was the multitudes of people you are to preach the gospel to;
the falling sheaves is what you see here to-night, the slaying
power of God. This is my power; I told you I would be with
you and fight your battles; it is not the wisdom of men, but the
power and wisdom of God that is needed to bring sinners from
darkness to light.' The Lord revealed wonderful things to me in
a few moments; my fears were all gone."

CHAPTER 20: LOVE & WAR

1. Carrie Judd Montgomery in her message "Life on Wings: The
    Possibilities of Pentecost," *Triumphs of Faith* (August 1912).
    Originally in a sermon she gave at Stone Church in Chicago in
    1910. Also found in Jennifer A. Miskov, *All Who Are Thirsty:
    Discovering the Fullness of the Holy Spirit* (Anaheim, CA: Silver
    to Gold, 2022), 84–87. Picture of Carrie Judd Montgomery
    used with permission from the Flower Pentecostal Heritage
    Center.

CHAPTER 22: FINDING YOUR PEOPLE

1. See Hebrews 10:23–25; James 5:16; 1 John 1:7; Acts 2.

CHAPTER 23: CULTIVATING REVIVAL IN FAMILY

1. See pages 133-140 in Miskov, *Walking on Water,* and https://jenmiskov.com/destinyhouse-history to learn more about the history and breakthroughs in Destiny House.

2. See our core values for Destiny House here: https://jenmiskov.com/vision-core-values and in the Appendix.

3. See a video of how one woman was healed of PTSD when someone who was living at Destiny House danced around her during one Friday morning worship time together: https://jenmiskov.com/blog/jessikatate.

4. See our core values for School of Revival here: https://www.schoolofrevivalfire.com/about and in the Appendix.

5. See the Appendix if you would like to read more about the core values of Destiny House and School of Revival.

CHAPTER 24: KEYS FOR SUSTAINING PERSONAL REVIVAL

1. See chapter 6: "Focus" in Miskov, *Walking on Water,* 72–80, which takes people through an encounter on connecting with God in silence.

CHAPTER 25: *HESED*

1. This quote is taken directly from an email exchange with Brian Simmons on the subject and dated 5/15/2023. Used with permission. This is the full quote: "*Hesed* is God's overflow of mercy, kindness, and love. It is limitless and extravagant.

Everyone on earth has the opportunity to experience this heavenly *hesed*. There is nothing you can do but receive it. It comes with no strings attached for those who are undeserving. *Hesed* took on human form in the person of Jesus Christ. He is *hesed* incarnate. I really believe that the inexpressible Hebrew word *hesed* is the greatest word in the Bible. There is nothing you can compare it to, and every definition falls short. It is an ocean of meaning in a drop of language. It is a word beyond words. It is a love past finding out. *Hesed* begs for paragraphs and parable to describe it. The love of a God who could never break a promise is what every heart needs. I am comforted completely when I ponder the revelation within the word *hesed*. Never doubt God's love. Never worry about His endless mercy to forgive you. Never hesitate to lean into His heart overflowing with *hesed*. It is love, kindness, faithfulness, tenderness, compassion, and mercy times infinity!"

CHAPTER 26: MIRACLE HOUSE

1. To see pictures and learn more about this story go to https:// jenmiskov.com/blog/miraclehome.

2. See more about the vision and heart behind Miracle House here https://www.jenmiskovministries.com/miraclehouse.

CHAPTER 27: FINAL BREATH

1. See pictures and videos of the Miracle Flight story here https://jenmiskov.com/blog/2014/6/2/miracles-come-when -you-have-no-other-options.

CHAPTER 28: TAKE THE FIRST STEP

1. See Nehemiah 4.

2. Though there are various reports that attribute the origins of this song differently, with none well documented, the song "I Have Decided to Follow Jesus" may have been inspired by a martyred Garo tribal man from Meghalaya (then a part of Assam) named Nokseng. The village chief became angry when he heard some from his tribe had been converted to Christianity. "He then called the family who had first converted to renounce their faith in public or face execution. Moved by the Holy Spirit, the man sung his reply, 'I have decided to follow Jesus. No turning back.' Enraged at the refusal of the man, the chief ordered his archers to arrow down the two children. As both boys lay twitching on the floor, the chief asked, 'Will you deny your faith? You have lost both your children. You will lose your wife too.' But the man replied, again singing, 'Though none go with me, still I will follow. No turning back.' The chief was beside himself with fury and ordered his wife to be arrowed down. In a moment she joined her two children in death. Now he asked for the last time, 'I will give you one more opportunity to deny your faith and live.' In the face of death, the man sang, 'The cross before me, the world behind me. No turning back.' He was shot dead like the rest of his family. But with the deaths, a miracle took place. The chief who had ordered the killings was moved by the faith of the man.... In spontaneous confession of faith, he declared, 'I too belong to Jesus Christ!' When the crowd heard this from the mouth of their chief, the whole village accepted Christ as their Lord and Savior." Whether this story is accurate and verifiable or not, we do know that many people are being martyred today because of their decision to follow Jesus. C.

Michael Hawn, "History of Hymns: 'I Have Decided to Follow Jesus,'" quoting (Stier, 2014, n.p. https://emailmeditations.com/2014/08/23/499-the-story-behind-the-song-i-have-decided-to-follow-jesus). Accessed January 5, 2023, https://www.umcdiscipleship.org/articles/history-of-hymns-i-have-decided-to-follow-jesus. See Hawn's article for various other origins attributed to the song and also *Why God, Why?* by Dr. Peramangalam Job, the key source that shares this martyrdom as the origin story. Read more at https://www.staddonfamily.com/2015/07/30/why-god-why-by-dr-p-p-job. Accessed January 5, 2023.

APPENDIX RELATIONSHIP ALIGNMENT EXERCISE

1. See https://jenmiskov.com/blog/2015/07/11/2015711awakening-europe-nurnberg-germany-day-2-running-to-jesus.

2. See https://www.schoolofrevivalfire.com or https://pioneeringrevival.jenmiskov.com/collections for a list of modules to explore going through together. Many also include a book study. Some that might be good are Walking on Water, Family Is the Fireplace of Revival, Writing in the Glory, Pioneering Revival, Holy Spirit, Consecration, Martyrdom, and more!

ABOUT
THE AUTHORS

JENNIFER A. MISKOV

Jennifer A. Miskov, PhD, is a revival historian, writing coach, and itinerant minister who loves to lead people into life-changing encounters with Jesus and invite them to experience a fresh baptism of the Holy Spirit and fire. She is the founding director of School of Revival, which helps equip and raise up yielded lovers of Jesus around the world. She taught at Vanguard University, The King's University, Bethel School of Supernatural Ministry, and other schools before diving full time into leading School of Revival (established in May 2020). She regularly facilitates Writing in the Glory Workshops around the globe to catalyze authors to write their first books. In addition to supporting Bill Johnson in his *Defining Moments* book, she has authored *All Who Are Thirsty, Fasting for Fire, Walking on Water, Ignite Azusa, Writing in the Glory, Life on Wings, Spirit Flood, Silver to Gold,* and more. She is ordained by Heidi Baker with Iris Global and currently lives in Southern California. You can learn more at JenMiskov.com.

Heidi Baker's greatest passion is to live in the manifest presence of God and to carry His glory, presence, and love to His body and a lost and dying world. She longs to see others laying their lives down for the sake of the Gospel and coming home to the Father's love. Rolland and Heidi founded Iris Ministries, now Iris Global, in 1980. In 1995, they were called to the poorest country in the world at the time, Mozambique, and faced an extreme test of the Gospel. They began by pouring out their lives among abandoned street children, and as the Holy Spirit moved miraculously in many ways, a revival movement spread to adults, pastors, churches, and then throughout the villages across Mozambique's ten provinces. Heidi is now "Mama Aida" to thousands of people and oversees a broad holistic ministry that includes a university, Bible schools, medical clinics, church-based orphan care, well drilling, food aid, primary and secondary schools, farms, widows' programs, and outreaches involving a network of thousands of churches and prayer houses. She earned her BA and MA degrees from Southern California College (now Vanguard University) and her PhD from King's College London. Heidi is calling for a passionate tribe of true believers in Jesus who will pour out their lives for love's sake, empowered by the Holy Spirit to bring people of all ages home to the Father's embrace. Learn more at IrisGlobal.org or rollandheidibaker.org/heidi-baker. See also her biography at https://rollandheidibaker.org/heidi-baker.

OTHER BOOKS BY
JENNIFER A. MISKOV

All Who Are Thirsty: Discovering the Fullness of the Holy Spirit with Heidi Baker and Carrie Judd Montgomery (Anaheim, CA: Silver to Gold, 2022)

Fasting for Fire: Igniting Fresh Hunger to Feast Upon God (Shippensburg, PA: Destiny Image, 2021)

Walking on Water: Experiencing a Life of Miracles, Courageous Faith, and Union with God (Bloomington, MN: Chosen, 2017)

Ignite Azusa: Positioning for a New Jesus Revolution with Heidi Baker, Lou Engle, and Bill Johnson (Redding, CA: Silver to Gold, 2016)

Defining Moments: God-Encounters with Ordinary People Who Changed the World by Bill Johnson with Jennifer A. Miskov (New Kensington, PA: Whitaker House, 2016)

Writing in the Glory: Living from Your Heart to Release a Message That Will Impact the World (Redding, CA: Silver to Gold, 2015)

Life on Wings: The Forgotten Life and Theology of Carrie Judd Montgomery (1858–1946) (Cleveland, TN: CPT Press, 2012)

Silver to Gold: A Journey of Young Revolutionaries (Birmingham, UK: Silver to Gold, 2009)

FOR MORE INFO:
JenMiskov.com/Store

ONLINE COURSES &
IN-PERSON TRAININGS
AVAILABLE BY
JENNIFER A. MISKOV

- Writing in the Glory
- Walking on Water
- Family Is the Fireplace of Revival
- Ignite Azusa
- Pioneering Revival
- Consecration
- Harvest
- Holy Spirit
- Revival: Past & Present
- Fasting for Fire
- Healing & Deliverance
- Martyrdom
- And more!

For more info:
SchoolofRevivalFire.com

From
Jennifer A. Miskov

Fasting is about feasting on more of God!

When many hear the word *fasting*, they immediately think of what they have to give up.
But what if fasting is more about *gaining* God than giving up?
What if fasting is a sacred doorway into fresh encounters with the all-consuming fire of God?

Author and revival historian, Jennifer A. Miskov, has tapped into an ancient pathway to divine encounter. She has given her life to studying how the great pioneers of revival experienced dynamic moves of the Holy Spirit, both in their personal lives and in the corporate church.

One of the key common denominators is fasting. Historically, fasting was never a formula for holiness or a means to manipulate God. In fact, in revival history, "the fasting ones" were actually "the feasting ones"—those who single-mindedly aligned themselves with what heaven wanted to release into the earth.

Featuring easy-to-follow fasting exercises, Scripture meditations, reflection questions, activations, and special chapters by Randy Clark and Lou Engle, *Fasting for Fire* will stir you to pursue the presence of God with more passion and zeal than ever before!

Purchase your copy wherever books are sold

From

Heidi Baker

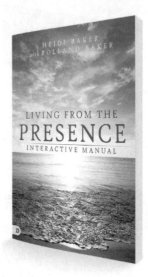

Experience the Supernatural Presence of the Holy Spirit in Every Area of Your Life!

Every follower of Jesus has received the Holy Spirit. If you have given your life to Christ, you have His very presence living inside of you.

And yet, there is still more!

What if the same Spirit who lives inside of you could work through you with miraculous power? What if the Holy Spirit was more than a theological concept and became your day-to-day supernatural experience?

In *Living from the Presence,* Heidi and Rolland Baker take you on a journey like never before. In eight interactive study sessions, Heidi and Rolland guide you into the manifest presence of God where you will encounter Him face to face and be forever marked by His transforming power.

Having the Holy Spirit live inside of you is an incredible honor; however, in order to walk out a lifestyle of supernatural power, you need to learn how to partner with the Spirit and see His manifest presence *rest upon you every day!*

Purchase your copy wherever books are sold

From

Heidi Baker

You Were Made For This!

From the remote corners of the jungle to the world's largest cities, the Spirit of God is powerfully at work within the hearts of people from all walks of life, drawing them to Himself. The harvest is abundant!

But where are the harvesters?

God is seeking workers for the harvest. He is raising up a new breed of missionaries to usher in the nations!

Discover your unique role in this great ingathering of nations!

Wherever you find yourself today—whether you are a student, executive, worker, parent, pastor, or missionary—you are in an exclusive and divinely appointed position to release the radical love and supernatural power of Jesus into your world.

You have been created for this purpose—to bring in the great harvest of nations.

It all begins with a choice: will you answer God's call?

Purchase your copy wherever books are sold

From
Todd Smith

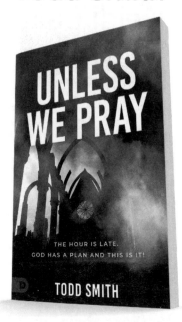

Our world, increasingly ravaged by darkness, is in desperate need for much more than human solutions. We need true spiritual power and authority to break through. Now is the time for the Lion of Judah to roar through His people!

Pastor Todd Smith has witnessed tens of thousands of lives supernaturally transformed by the power of God as he has stewarded the North Georgia Revival in Dawsonville, Georgia. As people attend their revival gatherings and experience water baptism, documented miracle healings take place, irreconcilable relationships are restored, prodigals return to God, and the impossible become possible in one divine encounter.

But revival doesn't just happen. There is a secret behind it.

Pastor Todd shows how sustained revival, supernatural power, and divine encounter are directly connected to prayer. In short, power-packed chapters, you will receive tools, weapons, and strategies that arm you for victorious prayer!

Don't let the forces of darkness continue to reign. Now is the time to enter into earth-shaking, darkness-shattering, Kingdom of God-advancing prayer!

Purchase your copy wherever books are sold

From
Todd Smith

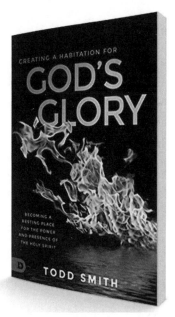

Become a Resting Place For God's Presence and Power!

Historically, God has moved mightily through revivals, awakenings, and outpourings of His Spirit. But these legendary moments are only a glimpse into what God desires for you each and every day.

Your everyday life can be a permanent dwelling place for God's presence.

Todd Smith, pastor of Christ Fellowship Dawsonville and leader of the North Georgia Revival, has firsthand experience in creating a habitation for God. He was on the verge of quitting the ministry when the Holy Spirit began showing him how to create a place in his life for the presence of God to live.

Discover the supernatural power and peace that comes when you make your life a habitation for God's glory!

Purchase your copy wherever books are sold

YOUR
Prophetic
COMMUNITY

Sign up for a **FREE** subscription to the Destiny Image digital magazine and get awesome content delivered directly to your inbox!

destinyimage.com/signup

Sign up for Cutting-Edge Messages that Supernaturally Empower You

• Gain valuable insights and guidance based on biblical principles
• Deepen your faith and understanding of God's plan for your life
• Receive regular updates and prophetic messages
• Connect with a community of believers who share your values and beliefs

xperience Fresh Video Content that eveals Your Prophetic Inheritance

eceive prophetic messages and insights
onnect with a powerful tool for spiritual growth and velopment
tay connected and inspired on your faith journey

Listen to Powerful Podcasts that Propel You into God's Presence Every Day

• Deepen your understanding of God's prophetic assignment
• Experience God's revival power throughout your day
• Learn how to grow spiritually in your walk with God

In the Right Hands, This Book Will Change Lives!

Most of the people who need this message will not be looking for this book. To change their lives, you need to **put a copy of this book in their hands.**

Our ministry is constantly seeking methods to find the people who need this anointed message to change their lives. **Will you help us reach these people?**

Extend this ministry by sowing three, five, ten, or *even more* books today and change people's lives for the better! Your generosity will be part of catalyzing the Great Awakening that many have been prophesying and praying for.